1000 HANDY HOUSEHOLD HINTS

1000 HANDY HOUSEHOLD HINTS

Lizzie Evans
Jean McGlone
Daphne Metland
Joyce Robins

OCTOPUS BOOKS

Contents

Don't Spoil the Ship for a Ha'porth of Tar

Strike While the Iron is Hot

There's Many a Slip 'Twixt Cup and Lip

Waste Not, Want Not

Many Hands Make Light Work

This edition published in 1989 by
Octopus Books Limited
a division of the Octopus Publishing Group
Michelin House, 81 Fulham Road, London SW3 6RB

© 1986 Hennerwood Publications Limited

ISBN 0 7064 3884 1

Printed in Czechoslovakia

50411

Illustrations by Advertising Arts and Stan North

"A Stitch in Time Saves Nine"

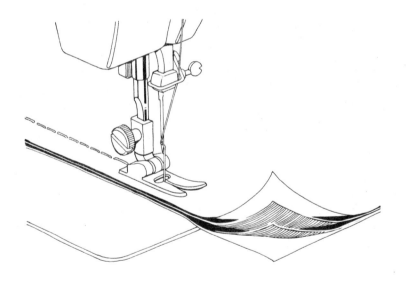

Tips on handiwork, household maintenance and plants

Knitting and sewing tips

NOTES FOR KNITTERS

Secure stitches: If you are slipping some stitches off your knitting needle, hold them secure by threading a pipe cleaner through them. The ends can be bent under so the stitches do not slip off.

Clothes peg clamp: Keep a large spring clothes peg with your knitting. When you stop temporarily, clamp the needles together with it. This will keep stitches from slipping off and your work becoming unravelled.

New for old: Re-use knitting wool from discarded sweaters by winding it tightly round a piece of wood or stiff cardboard, then dipping it in lukewarm water. Leave it to dry naturally and it will lose all its kinks.

Quick measure: Mark one of your knitting needles with coloured nail varnish into inches or centimetres, it saves hunting for the tape measure.

Back into shape: Plastic knitting needles that have gone out of shape can be straightened if you either hold them in the steam of a boiling kettle or plunge them in near-boiling water, then when you take them out of the steam or water you will be able to straighten them between your fingers. Put them into cold water immediately afterwards to set the shape.

Wool in order: Keep your knitting wool pristine by putting it in a plastic freezer bag with a loose elastic band around the top. If you're using several colours at once, use a plastic bag with small holes in it and thread the different wools through them. They will stay untangled that way. Single balls of wool can also be put in a small cardboard box. Make a hole in the lid for the wool to go through, then seal the box with sticky tape.

Light on dark: Use light needles when you knit or crochet dark yarn, dark needles with light. It is much easier to count the stitches that way and doesn't strain your eyes.

Instant information: When you buy wool, wind a small piece round one of the printed wrappers and put it on one side. Then if you need to buy some more you have instant information to hand, to take to the shop with you.

Look – no join: To make an inconspicuous join in knitting wool, thread a darning needle up from the new skein and darn the wool in and out of several inches of the old yarn. Remove needle, pull straight, then twist between the palms of your hands for a smooth look.

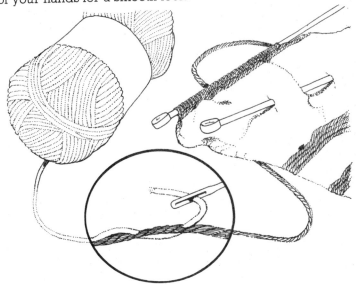

Untangled yarns: If you are knitting with two strands of yarn at once, thread the ends together through an empty cotton reel before you start. It keeps them smooth and untangled.

Lining up seams: When stitching together two large pieces of knitting or crochet, mark the seams first at intervals with coloured wool tags, so that you can line them up like seam notches to check that both sides are even.

Hook replaces needle: Use a crochet hook instead of a needle to 'sew' up side seams in textured or knobbly knitted garments.

Cuffs in place: Sew a couple of rows of spool elastic thread through the cuffs of heavy knit sweaters with a running stitch, then if you push up the sleeves, they will stay put.

MONEY SAVERS

Bird patterns: Don't throw away bird or flower patterned fabric, cut the shapes out and use them to decorate plain curtains or covers.

Useful ends: Don't throw away nearly used reels of cotton. Use the thread for tacking seams or hems.

New sheets from old: Sheets that are worn in the centre can be cut in half and then turned sides to middle, joined and re-used.

Blouse and petticoat: When making a blouse for a school child, give it an extra long tail and it will act as a petticoat, too, under her skirt.

Shirts into pillowcases: Don't throw away old white shirts, the backs from two of them will make a pillowcase.

Patchwork pieces: Hunt round charity shops and jumble sales for clothes you can adapt for yourself or the children and for patchwork pieces.

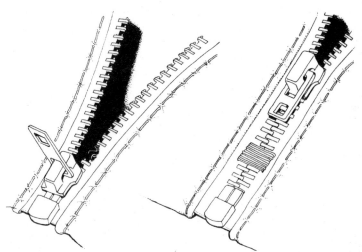

Mend a zip: If the zip fastener has broken at the base it can be salvaged: pull the slide down below the broken teeth, cut them out, then pull the slide up above the gap matching it on both sides. Stitch the zip together again just above the break.

Cushion stuffing: Use cut pieces of old knitwear, or cut up tights as a stuffing for cushions or soft toys.

Ironing board cover: The legs of pyjama trousers make good covers for an ironing board.

Button bank: Always save buttons and zips from discarded clothes.

Tape let down: Use iron-tape for the hemlines of children's dresses or boys' trousers. As the child grows, they are easier to let down that way. The tape will pull off easily after the garment has been laundered several times.

Extend a belt: A too-short belt can be lengthened easily if you undo it, remove the buckle, add a short length of narrow elastic to the buckle end, then replace it.

Woollen ties: Odd lengths of coloured wool can be crocheted into decorative chains to tie up Christmas or birthday presents.

Restore a tape: A limp linen tape measure can often be given a new lease of life if you iron it between two sheets of waxed paper.

Extend a hem: Make a horizontal tuck in the hem turn-up on children's dresses, or trousers, using the longest machine stitch: it will not show and can be let down later on as the child grows.

Extend a blanket: Blanket too short for the bed? Then sew a wide strip of discarded blanket of similar material to the bottom end, where it will be tucked in and unnoticeable.

New lining: Worn linings on otherwise good coats, jackets and skirts can be replaced. Carefully unpick the old lining, press out flat, then use as a pattern for a replacement one.

Flannel supply: Worn bath towels can be cut up and hemmed to provide a steady supply of flannels and face cloths.

Pretty napkins: Make a set of table napkins out of a worn tablecloth, edge them with decorative machine stitching.

Toddlers' pants: Discarded nappies can be turned into useful towelling pants for toddlers. Use two nappies per pair of pants.

Curtain hint: Switch your curtains around to opposite ends of the window every time you take them down for washing or cleaning, so that they keep their colour more evenly.

Add a band: If the hemline of a child's dress is too short for her, but the rest of it fits well, add a band of contrasting colour round the hem, team it up with a matching bow, buttons or belt.

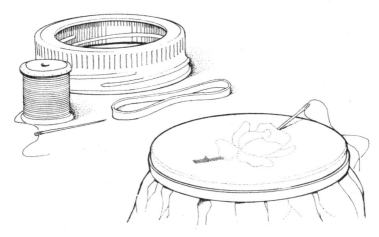

Embroidery frame: A metal fruit jar ring and an elastic band make a perfect miniature embroidery frame for small work.

Budget handkerchiefs: An old cotton shirt can be cut into squares and hemmed to make cheap handkerchiefs.

Needle sharpener: Blunt sewing machine needles can be sharpened if you 'stitch' them through a piece of sandpaper.

MACHINE SEWING

Fluff remover: Use a pastry brush to remove fluff from working parts of your sewing machine.

Curved seams: Use a shallow zig-zag stitch if you are machining curved trouser seams, it will take strain and wear and tear better than a straight one.

Stop the slip: To stop shiny fabrics from slipping off the table while you machine them, stretch a piece of towelling over the surface.

13

Slippery seams: When stitching seams on fine slippery fabrics, place a piece of paper underneath to make the job easier. The paper can be torn off afterwards.

Sewing jersey: All jersey fabrics should be sewn with the machine on a shallow zig-zag setting.

Useful bag: Fix a paper bag to the side of your sewing table top with masking tape or drawing pins, then scraps of fabric and cotton can be swept into it, and there is less clearing up to do afterwards.

Stray cottons: Use eyebrow tweezers to pull out stray pieces of cut cotton left in seams.

Sewing plastic: If you are sewing plastic, put it between a sandwich of waxed or greaseproof paper to make machining easier. It tends to stick otherwise. After the job has been done, the paper will tear away easily, leaving the stitching intact.

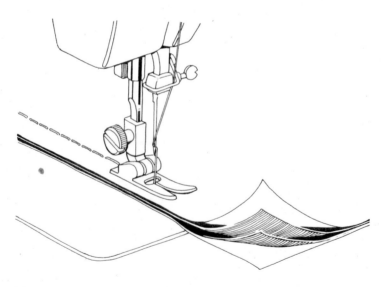

Tangled towelling: Looped fabrics like terry towelling will often get entangled between the needle and foot of the sewing machine. Avoid this by placing a sheet of tissue on top of the material before you start. It is easily torn away afterwards.

Machine seams for knitted garments: Use your sewing machine to seam hand-knitted or machine-knitted garments; use the loosest tension and a narrow zig-zag setting if your machine has one.

Eye in focus: Put a piece of white paper under the foot of your sewing machine when you are threading the needle, it makes the eye show up more clearly.

Surplus oil: Always stitch a few lines on a piece of blotting paper after you have oiled your sewing machine. This will blot up any surplus oil that might otherwise mark your fabrics.

Easy smocking: Mock smocking can be made easily on a zig-zag sewing machine: simply make four rows of gathers about $\frac{1}{2}$ centimetre ($\frac{1}{4}$ inch) apart, using a shirring foot with ordinary cotton, then embroider v's in a contrasting colour on it using the zig-zag stitch.

Breaking thread: If the top thread tends to break on your sewing machine, the tension is usually too tight. But it could be that you are using too fine a needle. If the bottom thread keeps breaking, it could be tight tension, which needs to be adjusted on the bobbin case, or you may have overwound the bobbin.

Powder for plastic: If you are top-stitching plastic material, smooth some talcum powder or French chalk over the area before you start, it will make it easier to work.

Be prepared: To save time when sewing a garment with a lot of seams, thread up two spools of cotton so you have a replacement ready when the first runs out.

Professional effect: Before sewing a decorative shell edging, or crocheting an edge on fine materials, take the thread out of your sewing machine, set it on the largest stitch length and run it along the edge. This will give you a row of minute, evenly spaced holes to guide you in getting a regular, professional effect with your stitching.

DRESSMAKING

Hem marker 1: A sink plunger marked on its wooden handle, makes a good hem marker for long skirts. It stands up by itself on the floor leaving your hands free to pin the skirt hem.

Hem marker 2: To mark a hemline, stretch a piece of string between two chairs, or a chair and table, at the desired height. Rub the string thoroughly with a piece of chalk, then put on the garment and turn slowly making sure the fabric brushes against the string all round. The chalk will mark the hem at the required spot.

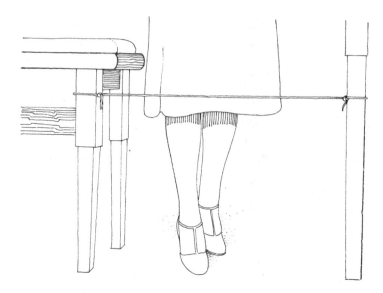

Nap in the right direction: If you're working with fabric which has a nap, like corduroy, mark the reverse side with an arrow to save sewing mistakes; use masking tape for the job, or stitch an arrow in contrasting cotton, chalk will tend to rub out. When the nap runs downwards, the colour appears lighter; if upwards the fabric looks darker.

Double thread: If you're working with double thread, knot each thread separately to prevent it pulling through. The cotton is much less likely to snarl up or twist.

Matching patterns: Match up stripes and tartans by turning the seam allowance under on one side and ironing it. Lay it alongside the seamline on the other piece, right sides upwards, matching it as you go and cover in place with transparent sticky tape. Stitch in the usual way, then remove the tape before pressing the seam.

Sewing scrap-book: Make a file or scrap-book of off-cuts of fabric and extra buttons from clothes that you make, for instant replacements if a button or a patch is required.

Hitting the spot: If you're putting snap fasteners on a garment, sew the projecting part on first, rub it with tailor's chalk, then press it against the side where the other half of the fastener is to go. It will mark the spot for you.

Heavy seams: Having difficulty in working with heavy material? Run a bar of soap along the wrong side of the seam before you start stitching. The needle will go through the fabric more easily and, when you come to press it, the seam will stay flatter.

Narrow belts: Iron-on hemming tape makes a good backing for narrow fabric belts.

Elastic threading: Attach a small safety pin to each end of the elastic when you are threading it through a waistline casing, that way you can monitor its progress as you pull it through.

Difference in arm measurements: When making a dress with a perfect fit, be sure to measure both arms for length and width. Many people find there is a difference between one arm and the other.

Shoulder straps: Sewing a dress with skinny shoulder straps? Then make another set of straps to sew over your bra straps, so they will be less noticeable.

Towel roll: Ironing the 'roll' into a tailored collar? Wrap a damp towel round a rolling pin and lay the collar over it to get the required curve. A padded rolling pin also makes a good sleeve board.

Removing pattern creases: Always iron paper patterns lightly before you use them to remove creases which might make them inaccurate.

Couture look: Give a couture look to a dress by making crochet covers for the buttons in sewing silk that matches the colour exactly. Use a double crochet stitch and either stuff with cotton wool until it is the right shape or stretch over a mould.

Scalloped finish: If you want a scalloped finish on a seam or hem, use rick-rack braid, letting only every other point show as you stitch, tucking the others into the seam allowance or up behind the hemline.

Heavy gathering: Use button thread on the bobbin if you are gathering heavy fabric by sewing machine. Loosen the tension first, do two rows on the longest stitch size available, then pull both sets of threads at once.

Sewing on patches: If you're sewing decorative patches or badges on to fabric, always glue them in place first with a dab of fabric glue, it makes them easier to work with. Failing that, spray the backs with spray starch, which will stick them in place while you sew, but will come out in the first wash.

Fabric loops: Always cut the fabric on the cross when making hand-made fabric loops, it will curve better and is much easier to sew.

Paper patterns: To make paper patterns last longer, spray them before you use them with a proprietary fabric protector.

Hemline hold-up: If you are hemming a fine fabric, use hairgrips to hold up the hemline while you are working on it, rather than pins, which would leave a mark.

Hold for pattern pieces: Use a clothes peg to hold pattern pieces together while you are working with them.

BUTTONS AND BUTTONHOLES

Correct tension: To avoid buttons being sewn on too tightly, separate the button from the fabric underneath with a matchstick while you stick it in place, or place a pin on top of the button between the holes so that the stitching goes over the pin at right angles to it.

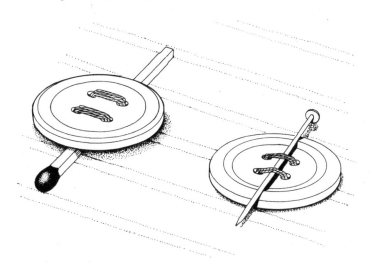

Fraying buttonholes: To stop buttonholes fraying while you stitch them, paint the cut edges with colourless nail varnish, allow to dry, then carry on stitching. Alternatively, mark the buttonhole in the first place with nail varnish and cut a slit through the centre when it is dry.

Long-life buttons: Dab the stitched centre of a button, front and back, with clear nail varnish before you wear a garment for the first time. The buttons will stay put much longer.

Buttons on shirts: The buttons on a tight fitting shirt will stay in place better if you sew them on with shirring elastic instead of thread. The same goes for the buttons on a button-through dress.

Button stitching: Buttons with four holes in them will stay put almost indefinitely if you stitch them, two by two, with separate lengths of thread. Then, if one side goes, the other should hold the button in place.

Button loops: Shoe lace makes good, inexpensive button loops.

DARNING, SEWING, AND EMBROIDERY

Use for off-cuts: Save long off-cuts of fabric from loosely woven material. When they are unravelled, they can be used as matching yarn for top-stitching, etc.

Tapestry repairs: When doing tapestry or needlepoint, tack some spare lengths of wool to the back of the work when you finish. They will come in handy later if you need to do any repairs to the work.

Templates: Cut patchwork templates from stiffened iron-on interlining instead of card, and use in place of heavy backing.

Threading a needle: Difficult needle threading is made easier if you spray hair lacquer on to the end of the cotton to stiffen it.

Fringe benefit: When making a fringe on the edge of a piece of fabric, mark the depth you require, then cut the fabric at intervals up to that point, being very careful not to snip across the vertical threads. The cross-threads stroke out much more easily if they are in short lengths.

Fine needle for beads: If you find you don't have a needle fine enough to take the beads you are threading, put a little melted candle-wax on the thread instead and twist it into a point before it hardens. Or, if the thread is really fine, paint some nail varnish on it and allow that to dry before using.

Curtain linings: When attaching curtain linings to the back of the curtain fabric, stop the stitches from going through to the outside of the curtain by putting a strip of cardboard between the two as you stitch.

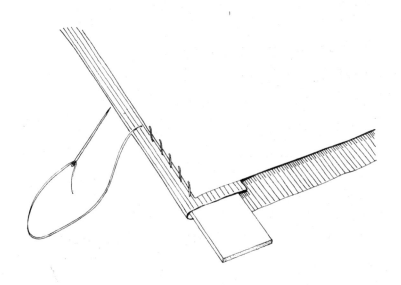

KNITTING AND SEWING TIPS

Hemming plastic: When working with plastic fabrics, turn up seam allowances and hemlines ready for stitching with sticky tape instead of pins.

Drawstrings: Always stitch drawstrings in place at centre back, so that they won't pull out accidentally.

Darning thread: Always use thinner rather than thicker thread for darning holes in fabric; heavy yarns tend to tear what is already a fragile, worn area.

Prevent snarling: To stop a length of sewing thread from snarling, always knot, or secure the end, which was nearest to the spool.

Large darns: Darn large items like sheets on the sewing machine; place a piece of paper underneath the hole and sew back and forwards over it, taking in the torn fabric edges until you have filled up the gap. When the fabric is washed, the paper will dissolve and the darn will remain intact.

WORTH NOTING

Pincushion: Stitch your pincushion on to a circle of elastic, so that you can wear it round your wrist as you work. Or stick pins and needles into a bar of soap, it lubricates them at the same time.

Quick check tape: A piece of worn tape measure stuck on to a sewing box, or the side of a sewing machine, is useful for quick check-ups on hem lengths, etc.

Jars for scraps: Small screw-top jars are useful for holding scraps of ribbon and lace.

Cut above plastic: Always cut out material on a plastic table cloth. The scissors move more easily over its slippery surface.

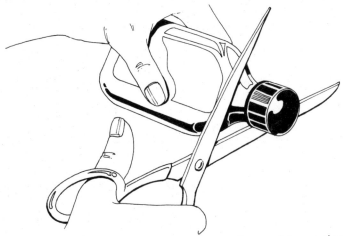

Scissor sharpeners: Sharpen scissors by making scissor movements round the neck of a sturdy glass medicine bottle or wine bottle. Or, cut through some glasspaper several times.

Red-hot needle: Use a red-hot metal knitting needle to poke holes into home-made leather or plastic belts, straps, etc.

Useful tail-comb: The tail from a tail-comb makes a useful instrument for poking out awkward corners or turning narrow tubes of fabric inside out.

Cushion settlers: If you are using small pieces of plastic foam as a cushion filling, add one or two larger pieces, this will stop the rest from settling down at one end only.

Finding an end: Push a drawing pin into the top of a reel of thread and wind the loose end around that. It is much easier to find.

Small things in store: Save matchboxes, then sticky-tape them together into a doll-size chest of drawers, to hold items like small pins, hooks, eyes, fasteners when you are sewing.

Cutlery tray: A plastic cutlery tray makes a good storage place for cotton reels and other sewing items.

Seam dampener: Use empty roll-on deodorant bottles (provided the ball is detachable), well rinsed out and refilled with water, to run along and dampen side seams before ironing.

Ever-ready needle: Push a piece of foam plastic into the centre of a cotton spool; use it to house a needle, ready for use next time.

Pins that grip: Before using pins on slippery fabric, poke them into soap: they will grip better that way.

Safety pin holder: Use a pipe cleaner to house safety pins – thread them on to it, then bend into a loop and twist the ends together. Large buttons can also be threaded on this way.

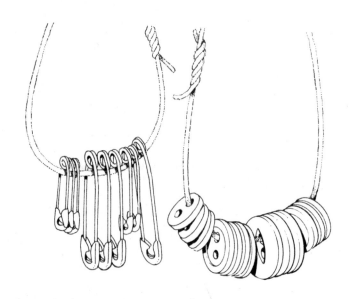

Instant mending: Keep an extra emergency sewing kit in the bedroom, so that buttons that are shed, hems that come down, whilst you are dressing, can be mended instantly, on the spot.

Darning mushroom: An electric light bulb makes a good darning mushroom for stockings and socks. The mushroom-shaped bulbs are heavier weight and therefore the best sort to use.

Money protector: Sew a small zip into the inside pocket of a child's jacket or blazer so that money and other items can be kept safely there.

Cover up: Making a dress to wear while entertaining or working around the house? Then make up an apron in matching fabric, so it is less noticeable when you wear it.

Long needle holder: Save a disused clinical thermometer case to house extra long sewing needles.

Slipping straps: To stop shoulder straps from slipping, run a couple of rows of machine stitching along them at shoulder-top level, using elastic thread in a matching colour.

Scissor store: Screw a cuphook to the side corner of your work table; it is useful for holding scissors which would otherwise tend to disappear under materials when not in use.

Pins to a magnet: Keep a small magnet in your sewing basket, it's ideal for quickly picking up spilled pins.

Filling for small items: Drained, dried coffee grounds make an ideal filling for very small items like pin cushions or tiny home-made toys.

Household maintenance

THE OUTSIDE

Unblock a drain: If you have no drain rods and must unblock an outside drain, you can sometimes save the expense of calling a plumber by using an ordinary garden hose with water flowing through it. Work from the dry side of the blockage and be sure to wash the hose thoroughly afterwards.

Clear gutters: In autumn, gutters tend to get clogged with leaves, causing overflows and blockages. To prevent the leaves from settling in the gutter, fix a strip of chicken wire along the top.

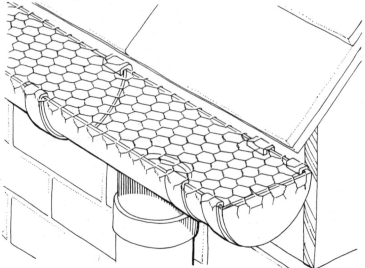

Damp detection: Mould or algae on an outside wall can be removed by scraping away, then washing the affected area with bleach diluted one to one with water. Leave to dry then repeat the bleach treatment the next day. If the mould reappears look for the source of the damp.

Window repair: Polythene sheeting can be used for an emergency repair to a broken window. To hold it in place without tearing, use thin battens over the top of the sheeting, with the nails passing through the battens and the polythene edge into the window frame.

PLUMBING

Burst pipes: Bandages and epoxy-resin adhesive can be used to repair burst pipes in an emergency. Mix up the adhesive according to the manufacturer's instructions and spread on the pipe and the bandage, then simply wrap the bandage tightly around the burst section of pipe. This should last long enough for you to get a plumber.

Thawing pipes: Don't use a blow torch to thaw frozen pipes – unless you're very careful you'll damage the pipe or even set fire to the house. Instead use a hair dryer, a hot water bottle, or cloths wrung out in hot water.

Avoid blockages: Never throw fatty or greasy food into the sink, this causes blockages.

Clearing a drain: If all else fails, try clearing a blocked drain like this. First pour down two kettles of boiling water, then a small amount of paraffin. Leave for twenty minutes and then pour down another two kettles of water.

Mending a washbasin: As a temporary measure, a cracked washbasin can be repaired by sticking strips of linen tape to the outside and covering these with gloss paint. Heavy duty waterproofing tape, of the kind sold in hardware stores for temporary repairs to pipes, will also work well.

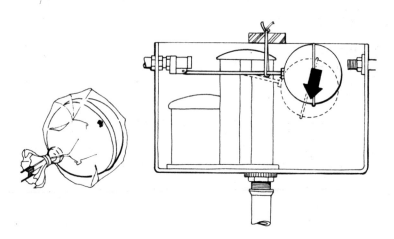

Punctured ball-floats: A plastic bag can be used to make an emergency repair to a punctured ball-float in the lavatory cistern – wrap the bag around the ball and seal with an elastic band. Cistern overflows can often be cured by bending the float arm downwards slightly. If the cistern itself is leaking you can cut the water off, while maintaining a supply elsewhere in the house, by placing a piece of wood across the tank and tying the arm float to this.

Cold tank insulation: When insulating a loft, remember that the cold water tank will now need insulating as well to prevent it from freezing. Never place insulation underneath the tank as this will cut it off from warmth from the rest of the house.

Repair a plumbing joint: A leak in a plumbing joint may be caused by worn threads. Undo the joint and wind a piece of cotton tightly around one of the threads. The joint should then screw back to give a tight fit.

Stop that dripping noise: The noise from a dripping tap can be prevented by tying a piece of string between the tap and the plughole. The water will now run down the string without dripping.

Prevent freezing: In winter even the smallest amount of water in unlagged pipes can freeze and cause a blockage. To prevent this, keep basin and bath plugs in place, especially at night.

HANDY THINGS TO KNOW

Fill that gap: Small gaps between door and window frames and the surrounding wall can be sealed with a flexible filler. For larger gaps, partially fill with old newspaper, then cover with filler.

A door that sticks: If a door sticks, find the offending area using carbon paper. Place some with the carbon side facing the inside of the door, on the frame and close the door. Repeat this, working your way around the door. The black marks will show where the door is rubbing. Sand the offending areas down, or just lubricate by rubbing with a candle.

Stiff lock: To free a lock that has jammed, smear the key with a little petroleum jelly and jiggle it about in the lock. A lock that is simply stiff can be lubricated by rubbing the key with a pencil, then working the graphite into the lock in the same way.

Preventing scratches: Regular use of a plastic washing up bowl prevents cutlery from chipping and scratching your sink.

Ending a squeak: A squeaky floorboard can sometimes be cured by lubricating the edges with talcum powder.

Smooth moving door: Soap can be used to silence a creaking door (just rub a little into the hinges) and make tight fitting drawers run smoothly (rub along the top and bottom edges.

WALLPAPERING

Symbols: These international symbols are now beginning to appear in wallpaper pattern books and on product labels:

〰	spongeable	⊞┝	paste-the-wall
≋	washable	▶|○	free match
≋	super-washable	▶|◀	straight match
▰	scrubbable	▶|◀	offset match
☀	sufficient light fastness	50 cm / 30	design repeat distance offset
☀	good light fastness	▐⟩	duplex
▌↘	strippable	〰≡〰	co-ordinated fabric available
▌↘	peelable	↑	direction of hanging
⌣∂⟋	ready pasted	↓↑	reverse alternate lengths

How many rolls of wallpaper do you need?: Standard wallpapers come in rolls approximately 10.05 m (11 yards) long and 530 mm (21 inches) wide. The chart gives the number of rolls required according to the height of the walls and the distance round the room. Allow extra for matching patterns.

NUMBER OF ROLLS REQUIRED

Distance around the room (doors and windows included)	WALLS Height from skirting →	2.15–2.30 m (7'–7'6")	2.30–2.45 m (7'6"–8')	2.45–2.60 m (8'–8'6")	2.60–2.75 m (8'6"–9')	2.75–2.90 m (9'–9'6")	2.90–3.05 m (9'6"–10')	3.05–3.20 m (10'–10'6")
30 m (98')		13	14	15	15	16	17	19
28 m (94')		13	13	15	15	15	16	18
27 m (90')		12	13	14	14	15	16	17
26 m (86')		12	12	14	14	14	15	16
24 m (82')		11	11	13	13	14	14	16
23 m (78')		10	11	12	12	13	14	15
22 m (74')		10	10	12	12	12	13	14
21 m (70')		9	10	11	11	12	12	13
19 m (66')		9	9	10	10	11	12	13
18 m (62')		8	9	10	10	10	11	12
17 m (58')		8	8	9	9	10	10	11
16 m (54')		7	8	9	9	9	10	10
15 m (50')		7	7	8	8	9	9	10
14 m (46')		6	7	7	7	8	8	9
13 m (42')		6	6	7	7	7	8	8
12 m (38')		5	6	6	6	7	7	8
10 m (34')		5	5	5	5	6	6	7
9 m (30')		4	5	5	5	6	6	6

31

Plant
and garden tips

IN THE GARDEN

Storing tools: When putting garden tools away for the winter, coat the metal parts with oil then bury them in a bucket of sand. This will keep rust at bay.

Hose handle: A short length of old garden hose can be split down the middle and slipped over the handle of a metal bucket to protect your hands.

Handy tool holders: Use a length of old hose to make handy tool holders for the garden shed or workroom. Cut off a piece 50 mm (2 in) long, then slit it along its length with a sharp knife. Nail it to a wall or piece of board and use like a spring clip.

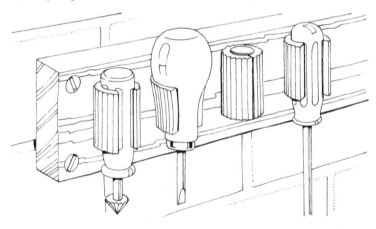

Bring on the plants: When replacing windows, save the old glazed frames. Propped against a wall, they make ideal cold frames for the garden to bring plants on ahead of the season.

Foil the elements: Protect young trees from the elements in winter by wrapping the length of their trunks in kitchen foil.

CUT FLOWERS

Trimmed and fresh: To keep flowers fresh as long as possible, change the water and cut off a small piece of the stems every day. If the stems are hard and woody (rose stems, for example), they should be crushed at the ends to encourage the absorption of water.

Charcoal in the water: If you can't change the water every day, put a piece of charcoal or a copper coin in the water with the flowers.

The long and the short of it: Flowers with short stems can be made to stand properly in a tall vase if the bottom of the vase is filled with screwed-up newspaper.

Lower leaves: Do not allow the lower leaves of flowers to trail in the water: remove them. If you leave them in the water they will rot and the flowers won't last as long as they should.

Mint green: When arranging flowers, consider using sprigs of fresh herbs, such as mint, thyme or rosemary for greenery – that way an extra fragrance will be provided, as well as extra colour.

Odds and evens: If you are arranging a small number of flowers it is easier with an odd number than an even.

Longer-lasting tulips: To make tulips last longer, make a series of small holes down the whole length of their stems.

Clear water: To keep a flower vase free from slime and to avoid the stale smell that can be caused by flower water, add just a few drops of bleach to the water. This will not harm the flowers.

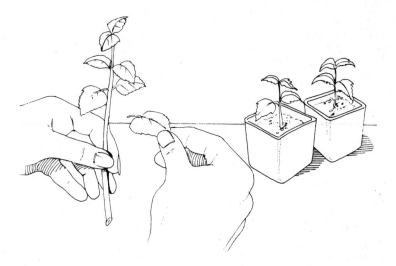

INDOOR PLANTS

Taking cuttings: Many plants can be grown quite easily from cuttings. They make ideal gifts or you can arrange to trade cuttings with your friends. The easiest method is by stem cutting. Select a plant with a soft stem. Pick a young shoot that is about 50 mm (2 in) long, choosing one with several leaf nodes (places from which leaves sprout). Make the cut with a sharp knife just below one of the nodes. Gently pull off the leaves from this node. Plant in a cutting mixture.

Shiny leaves: Polish heavy-leaved indoor plants, such as rubber plants, with cotton wool soaked in olive oil or milk.

Good mulch: Old tea-leaves, emptied on to the soil around houseplants, make a good mulch.

Ready together: When growing mustard and cress together, start the cress off three or four days before the mustard – if you do this they'll be both ready at the same time.

Plant drainer: Save broken crockery and use it at the bottom of plant pots to provide proper drainage.

Holiday care: Before going on holiday, put your plants in the bath with a little water and cover the top of the bath with polythene, leaving a few gaps to let the air in. Draw the curtains if the sun is likely to reach them through the window. The polythene cover maintains a moist atmosphere for the plants.

Miniature indoor gardens: Use hollow or ornamental bricks as miniature indoor gardens. Stand on a tile or tray before filling the gaps with earth and planting. Choose plants that all require the same treatment.

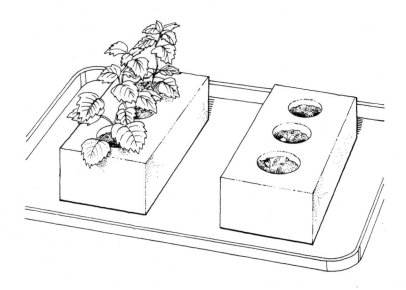

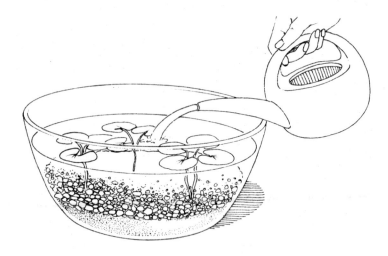

Indoor water gardens: To make an indoor water garden, plant miniature water lilies in 50 mm (2 in) of ordinary soil in a bowl (a transparent bowl is best). Cover the soil with a thin layer of gravel. Increase the depth of water as the plants grow.

POT PLANT PROBLEMS

The following is a selection of hints to help you deal with the most common houseplant problems. It is a good idea to check over your plants in spring and weed out those which have not survived the winter successfully.

Plant not growing: In winter it is quite normal for plants not to grow. If the plant is not growing in spring, the most likely reason is that it has grown too big for its pot. Otherwise it may be underwatered or underfed.

Spindly growth: When a plant grows very tall and spindly with only a few leaves, it means that it has been given too much food and water for the amount of light available. This happens most often in spring, when there is little light about. Cut down on feeding and watering.

Plant growing crooked or twisted: If you look carefully at a plant which has grown twisted, you will see that it has done so in order to get nearer to a source of light. Move the plant so as to give it more light. If the plant is already in plenty of light, turn it regularly, so that the whole plant gets the same amount of light.

Leaves dropping: If the leaves are old, the most likely cause of them dropping is underwatering. If the leaves are fairly young and they turn yellow before dropping, the cause is probably overwatering.

Yellow leaves: If the leaf is yellow but stays on the plant, then the cause is either that the plant is not getting enough light or that the soil or water contains too much lime. If the leaf drops the cause is overwatering.

Leaves loosing their markings: If a plant, which normally has leaves marked with pale cream lines or spots, is losing these markings, it is a sign that the plant is not getting enough light.

Browning of leaf edges: Overwatering, too much direct light or cold draughts, may all cause the edges of the leaves to turn brown.

"It's Not What You Do, It's The Way You Do It"

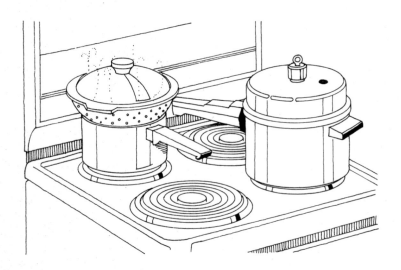

General household hints

General household hints

CLOTHES AND JEWELLERY

Anti-static: A dress that clings to your slip can be separated by running a wire coat hanger between the two as you are dressing. This cuts down the amount of static electricity, which is what makes them stick together.

Glove care: Leather gloves should be pulled off from the tip of each finger and stored flat, not screwed up one inside the other.

Hanging an evening dress: To hang up a long evening dress in the wardrobe without the hem scraping the floor, sew loops on the inside at waist level. Turn inside out and hang like a skirt.

Needles to hand: You can make a useful emergency sewing kit to carry in your purse, by cleaning out an old lipstick container and filling it with pins, needles and a spool of clear nylon thread.

Pack away: When packing a holiday suitcase, always put the heaviest items in first. If possible, put a layer of towelling between bumpy objects, like shoes, and your clothes.

Day-to-day care: Try not to wear any item of clothing more than one day at a time. Clothes last much longer, and look fresher, if they are given a chance to recover before being worn again. Always hang them up when still warm from the body, so that creases drop out.

40

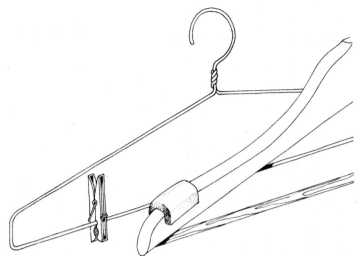

Non-slip: You can stop clothes from slipping off wooden hangers by sticking a piece of foam rubber at each end of the hanger.

Trouser hangers: To make hangers for trousers or skirts, without sewing on loops, fix two clothes pegs on ordinary wire hangers.

Inside-out storage: If possible store black items of clothing inside out to prevent them picking up dust and fluff.

Quick-dry Wellingtons: The inside of wet Wellington boots can be dried quickly with the aid of a hair dryer.

Wet shoes into shape: If leather shoes become thoroughly soaked, stuff them with dry newspaper before leaving to dry – if you don't, they'll dry out of shape.

Extended life: When shoes are new, put stick-on soles over the new soles. Make sure the soles are the right weight. The shoes will now last longer.

Leather costs more: Shoes with leather soles and heels wear out quicker and cost more to repair than plastic soles and heels.

Costume care: After a swim don't just wring a swimsuit out and put it away. Always rinse it in tap water first. The salt in the sea and the chemicals in swimming baths are very bad for material.

No perfume: Never put perfume or deodorant on clothes, both of them will damage the fabric.

Keeping in shape: To help garments to keep their shape, empty all the pockets and do up buttons and zips before putting away. Never put clothes in a wardrobe straight after wearing them – hang them up in the room for a few minutes first.

Roll don't fold: Clothes made of man-made fibres should be rolled rather than folded before putting away.

Real pearls: You can tell real pearls from paste by biting them – real pearls feel gritty. They should be worn as often as possible – contact with the skin helps to maintain their natural colour.

Jewellery cleaner: The impregnated cloths supplied for cleaning spectacle lenses are ideal for cleaning jewellery as well.

Brilliant detergent: Rhinestones can be cleaned by scrubbing gently with hot water containing a detergent, then drying with a soft cloth.

Away with tarnish: A coat of clear nail varnish will stop costume jewellery from tarnishing. Where the finish becomes damaged it can be repaired by rubbing with a stick of the metallic wax sold for brass rubbing in craft shops, then coating with clear nail varnish.

Novel necklace idea: Necklaces are easily damaged if they are jumbled together in a box; they tend to tangle, and getting any one out usually involves abusing the others. One solution is to keep them on a row of small nails or hooks along a dull stretch of wall. Not only will they be kept free from tangles, but you can see at a glance just what you have to choose from. They will also brighten up an otherwise unattractive area.

Linen or cotton: You can tell whether something is linen or cotton by placing a wet finger on the material. If the material is linen the mark will show through straight away.

Metal stains: Don't hang wet or damp garments on wire hangers – the metal can cause staining.

Stop the rub: If socks always wear out at the same point, rub a little paraffin inside your shoes at the offending spot.

Fluff remover: Use a piece of sticky tape wrapped around your finger, sticky side out, to remove dust and fluff from dark material.

Quick zip: A zipper that doesn't run smoothly can be lubricated by rubbing it with a soft pencil – the graphite does the trick.

Smooth metal: If your metal zipper tends to stick, rubbing it with wax will make it glide more smoothly.

Longer jeans: If you have to lengthen an old pair of jeans, remove the white line left at the fold by brushing on permanent blue ink (matched to the colour of the jeans) mixed with a little water.

Dyeing tip: When dyeing fabric in a washing machine, remember that it is much more important for the dye to circulate freely than it is for washing powder. So to be on the safe side, never dye more than half the manufacturer's recommended machine load.

Shoe shine: Baby oil makes very good shoe conditioner – rub some into the leather last thing at night and rub it off in the morning.

Potato buff: Badly scuffed leather shoes should be rubbed with a piece of raw potato before polishing.

Firm patches: Iron-on patches often do not have glue right up to the edges and this can cause them to lift off after a while. The solution is to trim around the edges till you reach the glue.

Hem creases: Use white vinegar to get rid of a stubborn hem crease – damp the material with the vinegar, then press flat with a warm iron.

Steam away creases: If you don't have access to an iron, you can remove the wrinkles from a garment by hanging it up in the bathroom while you have a bath – the steam makes the creases drop out.

Away with shine: Black clothing tends to become shiny with use – this can be got rid of by rubbing with a rag soaked in turpentine. Hang out of doors to remove the smell before wearing.

FURNITURE AND FURNISHING

Carpet pieces protect: Carpet samples make useful door mats. They are also useful for protecting table tops from typewriters, sewing machines, etc.

Even wear: A stair carpet should always be a little longer than the stairs themselves. You will need to move the carpet up or down from time to time and re-fix to ensure even wear.

No more wobble: If the rung or leg of a chair works its way loose, when sticking it back, mix a little sawdust with wood glue – this will keep it tight and stop it from wobbling.

Prevent yellowing: Table linen that is not in constant use should be wrapped in blue tissue paper. This will stop it from yellowing.

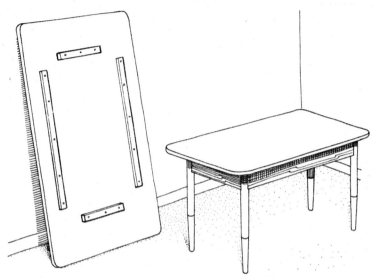

Plywood table top: When entertaining you can extend your dining table by putting a large piece of sturdy plywood over it. With the plywood in place, draw the outline of the table top on the underneath. Remove the plywood and fix strips of wood along the lines you have drawn, so that they fit just outside the original table top area. These will stop the plywood from sliding about when it's in place. Sand any very rough edges. Cover with a table cloth and no-one will be any the wiser.

Flat mats: Cloth table mats can be kept flat when not in use by hanging them on a clip board.

Good for brass – not for nylon: Although it's a good idea to lubricate old-style brass curtain tracks with a little light oil or petroleum spirit, never do this to nylon track or it will jam.

Top with brown paper: Where a bed has a wire spring base, it should always be covered with something, even if only brown paper, to prevent the springs staining the mattress.

Easy movement: An offcut of carpet slipped upside down under a heavy object to be moved will protect the floor and make moving much easier.

New top for old: Revive the look of an old coffee table by covering the top with a piece of material kept in place with a sheet of glass.

Rock – not slide: You will often find that a rocking chair will tend to slide about the floor when used. Keep it in one spot by glueing a strip of velvet (or velvet type) ribbon to the rockers.

No more curls: A rug that curls up at the edges can be kept flat by brushing the back with size. This sealant can be bought in decorating shops.

OUT SHOPPING

Buying a bed: The rule when buying a bed is 'buy in haste, repent at leisure'. Always check the mattress carefully before purchasing. Is it too hard, too soft?

Lists save time: Write shopping lists to correspond with the order in which you visit shops, in order to save time returning for something you forgot the first time around.

Resist temptation: Always take a list when you go shopping and stick to it. Supermarkets are designed to tempt you into buying things you don't really need.

Forward planning: If you have the space for storage, buying things that you will always need in bulk saves time, trouble and money.

Tempting price: Buy clothes in the sales in the shops to save money, but make sure you don't get carried away by tempting prices and start losing your judgement. Check seconds, or goods brought in for the sales, carefully for flaws.

Second-hand TV: If you are buying a second-hand television set, insist on seeing it working. If it is colour, try to find out why they are selling it. Ask if the tube is guaranteed. See the test card to check the colour balance. Second-hand black and white sets are temptingly cheap but be prepared to throw them away if anything major goes wrong; they are not worth repairing.

Shopping in the rain: Keep a sheet of polythene in your shopping bag to protect food in case of rain.

Heavy citrus: When buying citrus fruits, don't just judge the look of the fruit. Weight is the best guide – the heavier is normally the better.

HOUSE CARE

Fitting a duvet cover: When changing duvet covers, keep a couple of pegs handy. Get one of the far corners in place and peg it there, now do the same for the other far corner. Now locate the near corners (don't worry about what's happening to the rest of the duvet). Grasp the two nearest corners and give the whole thing a shake to straighten the middle out before removing the pegs.

Line up: When lining a shelf, cut several liners all at the same time. Put them inside the shelves one on top of the other and when the top one gets dirty, remove it and there will be another one underneath.

Fitted sheets: Save time and money by making your own fitted sheets – just tie a knot in the corners of an ordinary sheet and tuck this under the mattress.

Fingers off: Clear adhesive plastic stuck around switch plates and plugs will keep dirty fingermarks off the wall.

Anti-rust breadbins: Metal breadbins tend to rust at the bottom. To prevent this, glue small pieces of rubber under them to let the air circulate.

47

. . . and waste bins: A piece of self-adhesive plastic stuck to the inside bottom of a metal waste paper bin will prevent it rusting and staining.

Beat it clean: Never wash the cloth bag of your vacuum cleaner – doing so will allow dust to come through – beat it clean instead.

Dust avoidance: When hanging pictures, place a drawing pin at the top corners of each at the back. This holds the top of the picture slightly away from the wall and prevents the build up of dust.

AROUND THE KITCHEN

A firm board: To stop a pastry board from sliding, lay out a damp cloth underneath it. For a more permanent solution glue strips of rubber to the bottom of the board.

Softening a cork: If you wish to replace the cork in a bottle, but you find that it will not fit, soak it in a little hot water to soften it.

Keep under wraps: Soap lasts longers once it is in use if it is stored in a cupboard in its original wrapping for a while beforehand.

Flexible rubber: When you first fill a new hot water bottle, add a few drops of glycerine to the water. This makes the rubber more flexible and prevents it from perishing.

New knob: When a saucepan lid has lost its knob, replace it with a large piece of cork. Slip a screw through the hole and turn this so that it bites into the cork, holding it firmly in place.

Sharp knives: If kitchen knives are left in a drawer they will blunt each other. Keep them sharp by hanging them on a magnetic knife rack, but always store them handle downwards in case they fall.

Protecting glasses: To prevent glasses from cracking when hot water is poured into them, stand a metal spoon on the bottom before pouring.

Finding blunt areas: When sharpening a knife, look for blunt or worn areas by holding the edge towards the light. Where the knife is blunt it will catch the light and sparkle.

Foam lining: Line the inside of cutlery drawers with foam rubber to cut down on noise, wear and tear.

Magnet gloves: Oven gloves can be kept where they're most needed if you sew a small magnet as near to the outside of them as possible and use this to stick them to the cooker.

Bulletin board: Use the front of your refrigerator as a bulletin board – hold pieces of paper in place with small magnets.

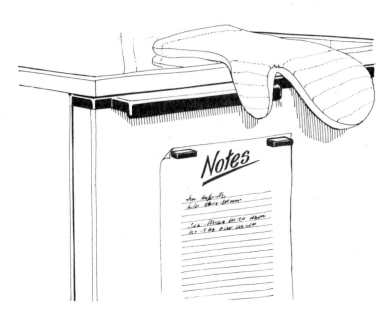

Coming unstuck: You can separate two glasses that are stuck one inside the other, by filling the inside one with cold water and immersing the other in warm to hot water.

Oil a stopper: To free the stopper from a decanter, put a little cooking oil around the stopper and tap gently around the outside until it comes free.

Easy reference: The insides of kitchen cupboards are an ideal place to stick metric conversion charts, favourite recipes – anything you need to have handy.

Lighting up: Damp matches can be made to light by dipping them in nail varnish and then letting this dry before striking.

Firm seals: If you seal a letter with a little raw egg white, it will make it impossible to steam open.

Stubborn lids: For a better grip on a stubborn jar lid, wrap a rubber band around it. If this fails, run a little hot water over the lid.

Better ice cubes: Air in water makes ice cubes slow to freeze. If you use boiled water, which has been allowed to cool, in your trays instead of water fresh from the tap, not only will they freeze quicker but the ice will be crystal clear.

Soup's up: When serving soup to the family, stir an ice cube into the children's bowls. It cools it to suit young mouths, and that way the whole family will be able to start eating at the same time.

No spills: When packing for a picnic, prevent salt and pepper from spilling by taping over the tops of the shakers.

String tidy: To keep string tidy, store it in a funnel. Hang the funnel up with the ball of string inside it and draw the string out through the end of the funnel.

Steel not wheel: Serrated or scalloped-edged knives should only be sharpened on a steel not in a wheel sharpener. Sharpen them only on the non-serrated side of the blade.

Use for egg cartons: Save a few plastic egg cartons for the children to use as throw away paint palettes.

See-through storage: Glass coffee jars, or translucent polythene ice cream tubs, are ideal for storing non-perishable foods. The ice cream tubs also make good freezer containers.

Clean milk bottles: Rinse milk bottles in cold water before washing in hot. Hot water will coagulate any remaining milk which, in turn, will stick to the inside of the bottle and be difficult to remove.

Prevent chips: Glue several strips of rubber to the top of your draining board to prevent plates from chipping. A rubber attachment on a tap will do a similar job.

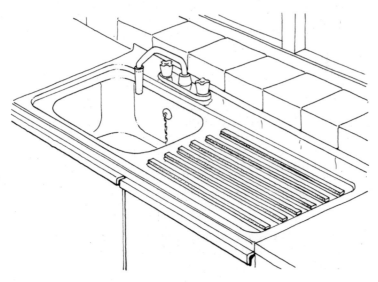

Spaghetti lighter: A piece of raw spaghetti makes a useful taper for lighting pilot lights or anything that's difficult to get to with a match.

No smoke wicks: Candle wicks will not smoke if they are soaked in a little vinegar, then left to dry before using.

Large into small: Instead of damaging candles that are just too big for a holder, dip the ends in a little warm water to soften them into a slimmer shape before inserting.

Sponges in good order: Sponges will become slimy if they are not allowed to dry out thoroughly after use. To revive a slimy sponge, soak it overnight in water containing a little vinegar. Wash the sponge thoroughly before using.

Longer life for rubber gloves: Rubber (not PVC) gloves are easily punctured by long fingernails. Prevent this by putting a piece of cotton wool in the end of each finger.

Stop steel wool rust: Steel wool will not go rusty if it's kept in soapy water. Make sure that it is completely covered with water.

ABOUT THE HOUSE

Placing pictures: If you cut the shape and size of a picture out of paper you will be able to select its correct position without having to make holes in the wall. When you come to mark the nail for the picture use a wet finger – it will dry without leaving anything that will show.

Straighten up: To cure a picture that will not quite hang straight, wrap some adhesive tape around the centre of the wire – this will stop the picture from slipping sideways.

Broken glass: A pad of damp cotton wool is just the thing for picking up tiny fragments of broken glass. Dab the affected area and the pieces of glass will stick to the pad which can then be thrown away.

Wet book: Dry a book that has been dropped in the bath by putting tissues in between each page. Repeat this procedure until the pages are nearly dry, then leave overnight with a sheet of paper between each page and press under a weight. Don't use too heavy a weight or you'll damage the binding.

Test for a damp bed: If you're not sure whether a bed has been properly aired or not, put a hand mirror between the sheets. Leave it for 10 minutes or so, if it has clouded over when you remove it, the bed is damp.

Smooth a chipped surface: Chipped glass and porcelain can be sanded smooth with very fine sandpaper.

Stopcocks and fuse box: Go around the house and mark the various stopcocks showing which way to turn them and what they do. If you do this now you'll be able to find the right one easily in an emergency. Do the same for your fuse box.

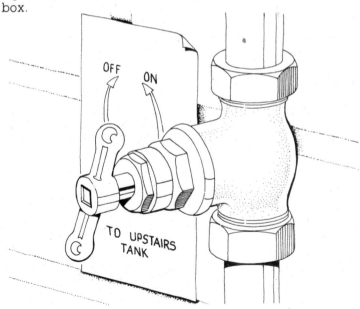

Preserving books: Hot dry air causes the binding of books to crack and the pages to yellow – keep them somewhere cool with a good circulation of air.

Keeping warm: Remember that cellular blankets will only keep you warm if they are sandwiched between you and an ordinary blanket, bedcover or eiderdown.

Threading a rod: Slip a thimble over the end of a rod that has to be threaded through the hem of a curtain and you will prevent it from catching in the fabric.

New candles for old: A broken candle can be repaired by softening both broken ends in a little hot water before ramming the two ends together and holding them there until the wax sets. Hot water will also soften bent candles sufficiently to allow them to be rolled straight on a table top (unless the candle has a delicate finish).

Freeze first: Candles will burn more evenly, and therefore last longer, if they are put in a freezer for a few hours before using.

Slow burner: A candle will burn more slowly, and can be used as a substitute night light, if you sprinkle the top with a little salt.

Safe glue: Flour and water mixed together to make a paste provides a good safe glue for young children.

Musty suitcases: To stop suitcases from smelling musty after they've been out of use for a while, put a few sugar lumps inside them before putting them away.

Coming unstuck: Stamps that have become stuck together will be easier to separate if you put them in the freezer for about half an hour.

Bouncing back: Restore a ping pong ball that has been dented by putting it in hot water with a little salt added.

Tidy cables: Keep electrical cables tidy by winding them into a loop and slipping this inside a cardboard tube.

Select stems: When you are selecting or arranging flowers, hold them at the bottom of their stems and not by the neck, where they are easily bruised.

Sugar revival: A dying fire can be revived by throwing a few handfuls of sugar on to it.

Seeing in the dark: Put a dab of luminous paint on light switches to make them easy to find in the dark.

GETTING IT ALL TOGETHER

'Wish you were here': Before you go on holiday, decide who you wish to send postcards to and write out names and addresses on sticky labels. This saves taking your address book, wasting valuable holiday time, and makes sure that no one is forgotten. Remember to pack the labels in your suitcase!

Wallet list: Make a note of names and numbers of all credit and identity cards kept in your wallet. If the wallet should get stolen you won't have the dreadful task of trying to recall precisely what was in it. Never keep bank cards together with your cheque book, it makes a forger's life too easy.

Help in a hurry: Save time by keeping near the telephone a list of numbers that are either needed very often, or in a great hurry.

Scribble board: Paint the wall near the telephone in a gloss paint to match the existing wall colour, and use a contrasting coloured crayon to scribble down notes and numbers. These can then be wiped off with a damp cloth.

Pound wise: Keep a one pound note in a pocket of your handbag for use in an emergency.

Spot a case: Spotting your suitcases when they come off the conveyor belt at an airport can be a problem, particularly if they are not very distinctive. Put a strip of brightly coloured sticky tape (the kind used to decorate bicycles) around them to make it easy.

A line in time: To make a neat alteration to a telephone book, write the information on a strip cut from a self-adhesive label. If you do this, and keep to a standard number of lines per person, it will save you eventually having to copy old numbers into a new book.

Prevent ageing: A clipping from a newspaper can be preserved and stopped from yellowing by soaking it for an hour in a saucer in which you have dissolved a milk of magnesia tablet in just a little soda water. Pat off most of the moisture then leave until completely dry.

Getting bags into shape: You can make polythene bags fit particular objects closely by cutting the shape of the object out of thick paper and slipping it inside a polythene bag. Sandwich the bag between two sheets of paper. Now, with a moderate iron, taking care not to go over the opening, the bag will seal itself around the shape you've cut and you can slip out the cut-out and substitute the object in question.

Long life wrapping: Store those bits of Christmas wrapping paper you can't bear to throw away in the long cardboard tube found at the centre of kitchen foil rolls. Iron the wrapping with the iron on low heat to remove creases, roll and insert into the cardboard tube. Now it's ready for next Christmas.

Addresses on file: Instead of using an address book, copy names and addresses on to a card file. That way alterations can be made easily and without mess.

Keeping things upright: A piece of elastic pinned to the front inside of a drawer is ideal for holding small bottles upright, when the drawer is opened or shut.

Silver wrapping: In an emergency, kitchen foil doubles as an attractive silver gift wrap.

On the scent: Use melted candle wax to seal the top of scent bottles, etc., before travelling – that way you can be sure of avoiding an accident.

A good tip: You can protect the tip of your umbrella and the inside of your umbrella stand by lining it with a piece of foam rubber.

NEW WAYS WITH FAMILIAR THINGS

Clear labels: To keep the instructions on prescribed medicine clear, coat the labels with colourless nail varnish straightaway. This will save them from getting smeared or fading.

Useful funnel: Cut off the top from a plastic bottle before throwing it away and you'll have made a useful funnel.

Sealing packets: Use clothes pegs to reseal packets of food temporarily.

Fire lighter: When lighting a fire, use a portable hair dryer as an electric bellows. Hold it some distance away from the fire and use with caution for short periods at a time.

Dry spot: When you have to wash a small part of a garment or remove a stain, dry the affected spot using a hairdryer to avoid leaving an unsightly ring (see also page 140).

Match a lock: Use different shades of nail polish to mark keys and the outside of locks to match. Then you won't have to go through every key on a ring before opening the door.

Pack a pleat: When packing a pleated skirt hold the lower end of the pleats together with paperclips.

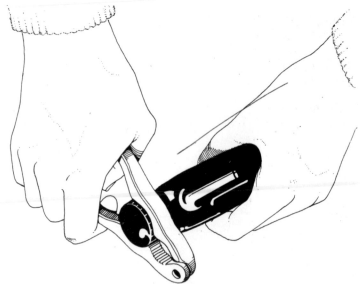

Getting a grip: A pair of nutcrackers can be useful for giving a grip on small bottle tops that won't move. Be careful not to use too much force though.

Frost protectors: Dry-cleaning bags placed over plants overnight will help to protect them from frost.

Mini crush: Use a pair of teaspoons, one inside the other, as a mini pestle and mortar when crushing medicine tablets.

Bath salts: Save large coffee jars to use as attractive containers for bath salts. Paint the lids a colour to match the bathroom, using acrylic paint for the purpose.

Wrap around: Self adhesive draught excluder is ideal for wrapping around anything (tennis rackets, for example) where you need a good grip.

Plant container: An old bird cage makes an attractive way of presenting plants. Trailing plants will look particularly good.

Rolling pin: A large wine bottle makes a very good rolling pin. Fill it with iced water and cork it firmly before using.

Display case: Use an old wooden cutlery box fixed to the wall to act as a miniature display case for small objects.

Short flowers: Use an old sauce boat as a vase for short-stemmed flowers.

Keeping the cats away: Chilli sauce makes an unusual cat repellant. To keep the cats off a surface, rub it with a little sauce then buff. (Don't try this with soft furnishings, only hard, washable surfaces.)

Battery corrosion: Fizzy drinks have all kinds of unusual uses. To remove corrosion where a battery has leaked, soak the affected area in a fizzy drink overnight, rinse and dry.

Corner dust: An old toothbrush, ready to be thrown away, is useful for getting dust out of awkward corners.

Rub off: If you haven't an eraser, try using a thick rubber band instead.

PARCEL POST

Avoid paper waste: The easiest way to cut just the right length of wrapping paper for a parcel is to wrap a piece of string around the parcel, cut this off and use this to measure the correct length of paper.

Safely tied up: Make sure your parcels stay done up properly. Before tying, dip the string in a little warm water. Tie the knot while the string is still wet. As the string dries it will contract making the knot extra tight.

Better safe . . . : When sending a parcel abroad, wrap and label it twice – then if the outer covering is damaged or lost, it should still reach its destination.

Cutting down on household chores

TIME SAVERS

Less leg work: When tidying the house, keep a basket in a strategic place, such as the foot of the stairs, so that as you go along you can put things in it that need to be taken up to the next floor.

Quick quilts: Use continental quilts, then you will find bedmaking quicker and easier.

Avoid ironing: If you smooth and fold clothes carefully when they come off the line, or out of the drier, you can keep ironing down to a minimum. You will not have to iron things like pillow cases, tea towels, sheets, etc.

Spread the work: Tidy up as you go along, it is much quicker than leaving it all to tackle at one time.

CLEANING AND POLISHING

Once a year: Furniture polish, applied to surfaces that do not receive wear, will last for a year and should therefore just need dusting from then on.

Wooden floors: Don't have hand-polished floors, they take time. Seal all wooden floors with a paint or wood sealer, so that they can be simply swept to keep them looking good.

Plastic pick up: As you go around the house, wear a small plastic bag tucked into your waist for picking up bits like drawing pins, hair pins, etc.

On the move: Keep a set of duplicate cleaning tools upstairs, to cut down on time. Have an extra long flex fitted to the vacuum cleaner, or use an extension cable, in order to let you go for a long period without unplugging.

Skirting dust: If you don't have a hose attachment to the vacuum cleaner and you want to clean near the skirting board, damp the fingers of your rubber glove and run them over the area. The dust should cling together into manageable lumps.

Clean as you go: Clean up stains and marks as you go. You will find they are much easier to remove immediately rather than later.

IN THE KITCHEN

Saves drying up: Invest in a good dish drainer, including a special cutlery basket, so that you don't have to do drying up after washing.

Wipe clean shelves: Cover shelf tops with stick-on wipe clean plastic covering, then they are quick and easy to clean.

Oven clean: When cooking roasts, place kitchen foil loosely over the joints. It cuts down on grease spatters and you won't have to clean the oven afterwards. Or, try cooking meat in special plastic roasting bags as they cut down on basting too, and cleaning the tins.

Non-stick: Use non-stick pans, whenever you can, to make washing up quicker and easier.

Out of sight: A dishwasher not only cuts down on washing up, but makes the kitchen tidier, since dirty plates are stacked out of sight immediately.

Scrape away: Use a plastic windscreen scraper for cleaning excess food off plates before washing up.

Warm whisk: A whisk, warmed by dipping in boiling water, will help to melt fat which is too cold to cream.

No last minute washing up: Use paper picnic cups and plates which you can throw away when you have your last meal before a weekend away or a holiday. This saves last minute washing up.

Quick wipe clean: When putting jam jars, sauce bottles, etc., away, wipe their bottoms to prevent them marking the shelf they stand on.

Keeping tastes apart: Use one side of a chopping board for onions and smelly chopping, and use the other for lemons and other items to avoid tainting. (See page 100 for how to get rid of smells.)

Contain those crumbs: Line the bread bin and other drawers that will contain crumbly things with foil or paper to help cleaning up afterwards.

Instant rubbish disposal: When preparing a lot of food in one go and therefore accumulating a great deal of rubbish, hang a carrier bag as near to the work surface as possible; on a floor unit door, for example. You can then sweep the peelings, crumbs, etc., into it straightaway, thus clearing up as you go along.

Oven shelves: If your oven shelves have badly burnt-on food, remove them and soak them in a bowl of biological washing powder and water overnight. They will be much easier to clean the next day.

Kitchen planning: One day, keep a careful watch on your movements in the kitchen to see how often you need to walk from one side to the other. If this seems to be too often, you will need to rethink your storage systems. Keep all much-used items, such as tea and coffee-making equipment, together and electrical appliances near the sockets.

THREE GOOD THOUGHTS

Better bikes: Put a thin coat of petroleum jelly on bicycles that are left out in the rain, to protect them from rust.

Powder container: To save making a mess when applying talcum powder on your feet, put a little into an old shoe box instead and step into the box.

Hairbrush care: Don't wash hair brushes with soap, instead use the same shampoo you use for your hair. It is much easier to rinse out afterwards.

Money savers

WASHING UP

Clean to dirty: To conserve water and detergent, always wash from the cleanest items to the dirtiest, whether it is clothing or crockery, pots and pans.

Too strong: Most people tend to use more washing-up liquid than they need – dilute yours to half strength with water whilst still in the container and save money.

Soap scraps: Save scraps of soap left over from bars to make into useful liquid soap Combine 300 ml ($\frac{1}{2}$ pint) of scraps with 300 ml ($\frac{1}{2}$ pint) of hot water and 3 ml ($\frac{1}{2}$ teaspoon) of borax. Mix well and leave to cool before using. (See also page 199.)

SHOPPING FOR FOOD

Bulk buying: Large amounts of goods usually work out cheaper, but don't lose your head; if the product is perishable and is likely to lose its flavour before you use it, don't buy.

Dented tins: Do not buy fruit or vegetable cans that show signs of leakage, or that look in very bad condition. Never buy damaged or dented cans of meat or fish.

No bargain: Some 'bargains' are not what they seem, such as jams that look as though they are 450 g (1 lb) jars but are, in fact, only 350 g (12 oz). The answer is always to check the weight on the label.

Hungry shopping: Don't shop when you're hungry or you'll find you've bought a lot more than you need.

Share the bulk: Buying in bulk really does mean buying huge quantities, for example, 4 litre (7 lb) jars of jam. So the best way is to form a co-operative and share the load a bit.

Supermarkets save: Large supermarket chains are almost always cheaper for groceries because they buy in bulk and package their own brands.

FRUIT AND VEGETABLES

Open markets: The cheapest places to buy fruit and vegetables are open markets. As long as you are prepared to bargain, you should get good quality, too. Don't accept inferior fruit from the back of the stall.

Go for fresh first: Fresh vegetables in season are almost always much cheaper than those that are frozen, tinned or dried.

POULTRY, MEAT AND FISH

Lean turkey: There's more lean meat on a turkey – 54% in fact, compared with 42% on chicken. Duck has more fat and only 33% lean meat.

Clean bones: Mince cooked chicken bones, both to clean the mincer and to provide the dog with cheap meal. Use the finest disc on the mincer and add bread to the bones as they go through.

More fish for less: Buy filleted fish – although it seems more expensive, it means you are not getting any wastage. The bones and head of most fish weigh surprisingly heavy.

Better bacon: Smoked bacon is more expensive than green but lasts longer. Buy bacon loose. Look for shops selling bacon bits, they are often a good buy. (See also page 66.)

Low fat mince: There are no regulations governing the amount of fat in mince. If you are worried, then select a piece of meat and have it minced for you or mince it yourself.

Home-made burgers: Most frozen burgers have only 80% meat content and are expensive; it is much cheaper to make your own.

Pork versus beef: Pork sausages have to contain 56% pork, so are more expensive than beef sausages which contain only 51% beef. The beef are less nutritious but very filling.

No cheap cuts: Buying cheap cuts of meat is often a false economy as they take more fuel, because they need longer cooking and often shrink a lot in the cooking.

Check on chickens: Fresh chickens may look more expensive to buy initially but contain 10% less water than frozen ones. Take this into account when comparing prices. Remember when calculating weight, only half of the chicken's weight is made up of meat. The other half is bones, giblets, etc.

Bacon for quiches: When using bacon in quiches, etc., don't use cut whole rashers. Buy bacon offcuts instead. These are perfectly good, they're just too small, or the wrong shape to be made into rashers. (See also page 65.)

FUEL SAVING

Cheapest fuel: Check with the Solid Fuel Advisory Service as to which is the cheapest fuel for your appliance. Buy as much as you can store in one go, out of season, when it is cheaper.

Maximum comfort: Set the time clock so that the heating comes on half an hour before you get up, and goes off half an hour before you go to bed. This provides maximum comfort at less cost.

Less than half price electricity: The Economy 7 tariff is particularly beneficial to those with water heating and/or electric storage heating since electricity used during seven hours overnight is less than half price.

Buy in summer: Buy heaters and other winter items in the summer when they are on special offer.

Save 8%: By turning the heating down by one degree Centigrade all year, you will save 8% of your yearly bill.

PREVENT HEAT LOSS

Foil the heat: Most radiators give off a fair amount of heat direct into the outside wall. You can make them much more efficient by sticking metal foil to the wall behind them.

Loft insulation: You can lose 40% of your heat through windows, floors and other gaps. Make sure that your loft is insulated – if not, see if you can get a government grant.

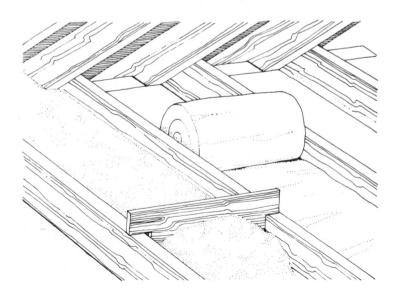

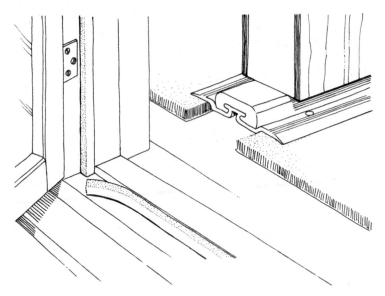

Stop that draught: Cut down on heat losses, use draught excluders around doors and windows – use thin plastic strips from ironmongers. Use a sausage type excluder at the bottom of the doors.

Flap a gap: Cover the gap in the door where the letter box is with a flap of material to cut out draughts.

Cover old fireplaces: If you do not use old fireplaces, then cover them with hardboard to keep the room warmer. Fit the hardboard out of sight in the chimney throat and drill a few holes in it for ventilation. Remember to remove it, though, if you change your mind and decide to have a fire.

AVOID WASTING HOT WATER

Hot running tap: Do not wash anything under a hot running tap with the plug out of the basin. It wastes money.

Bowl is better: Use a bowl for washing up, instead of the sink, and save on hot water.

Take a shower: A shower uses 29 litres (6½ gallons) of water compared to a bath which uses 90 litres (20 gallons).

Once a day: Reduce the amount of hot water you use by not doing the washing up after every meal. Stack it neatly in the corner of the sink, and tackle it once a day.

CAREFUL COOKING

Saucepans should fit: Make sure that the saucepan covers the electric ring, or that the flames of the gas are not licking around the edge of the pan, otherwise you are wasting energy.

One ring not two: Steam faster-cooking vegetables over slower vegetables – put them in a colander with a lid over a saucepan containing the slower-cooking vegetables. This saves using a second ring.

Less for pressure cookers: Use your pressure cooker whenever you can, it takes less fuel than conventional methods.

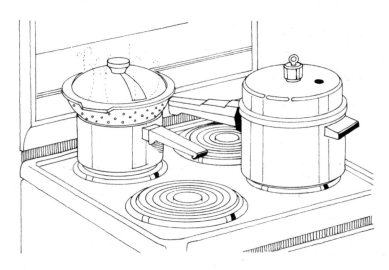

All together now: When you use the cooker, prepare as many dishes as possible to go in the oven together. Save up your baking so that you do a week's worth at one time, or get together with a neighbour and use each other's ovens in turn.

Just enough water: Never boil more water than you need in a kettle, but always make sure you cover the element with water in electric ones. Excess boiled water can be tipped into a vacuum flask to keep hot for the next cup.

One cuppa: If you only want one cup of tea, it is cheaper to boil the water on a gas ring than to use an electric kettle.

Early turn off: You can save energy when cooking a dish in the oven, for which the exact cooking time is not critical, by turning off the oven 15 minutes before you intend to serve.

SIMPLE SAVERS

'Log' fire: If you have an open fire, don't throw away old newspapers; not only can they be used for starting the fire, you can make them into 'logs' by rolling them up tightly and tying the ends with string.

Candle lighters: Save waxed milk cartons and the stub ends of candles. They make good fire lighters.

Foiled again: Kitchen foil can be washed after use with a little hot water and detergent, smoothed out, left to dry, and used again.

Restringing a necklace: Nylon fishing line is ideal for restringing necklaces – it's very strong and rigid enough to be used without a needle.

Long distance: Save money on long distant telephone calls by setting a time for the call on a kitchen timer before you start. Also make a list beforehand of any special things you want to say.

Cleaning windows: Don't waste money on special window cleaning preparations – old newspaper dipped in warm water works just as well.

Line with wallpaper: Use leftover wallpaper to line drawers and cupboards.

The last trace: You will find it easier to get out the last traces of toothpaste if you warm the tube before squeezing it.

Half a load is not better than none: Do not use dishwashers when they are only half full as this is a waste of water and money. Wait till you have a full load – items can usually be pre-rinsed while they wait.

Cooking for one: Save the foil containers in which some convenience foods are wrapped. They are a handy size for cooking small portions.

"If a Job's Worth Doing, It's Worth Doing Well"

All about cleaning

Quick tips for everyday jobs

Clean baths: Bath cleaner left in the bathroom, combined with your favourite method of bribery, nagging or persuasion will train the family to clean the bath and wash the basin immediately after use.

Better dusters: Your dusters will last longer and pick up better if, when they're new, you soak them in a solution of one part glycerine to one part water. Leave them to dry thoroughly before using.

Bubble bath: Bubble bath is a good investment for children as it saves having to clean the bath afterwards. It also cleans the children with the minimum of fuss.

Bag tidy: Before vacuuming, tape a small paper bag to the handle of the cleaner. Odds and ends, like paper clips, that the machine won't pick up can be dropped into the bag.

Dusting at the double: Instead of using a duster, slip an old sock over each hand when dusting and you'll get the job done in half the time.

A cleaning caddy: A caddy or tray containing polish, brushes and cloths can be carried around the house as you clean, and will keep everything to hand.

Clutter box: A clutter box is well worth having if there are children in the house. Choose a large cardboard box and stand it under the stairs or in the hall. After a quick daily tidy up, put all the books, gloves, shoes and miscellaneous family debris into it. When cries of 'Mum where's my book/hat/shoe laces' start, you can direct everyone to the clutter box.

Cobwebs: Remove cobwebs using a duster tied round the head of a soft broom.

Curtains: Curtains can be easily dusted using the vacuum cleaner attachment. This is worth doing regularly as dirt left in the fibre for long periods will rot it, with the result that the curtains fall to pieces when washed.

Doormats: When you use doormats, the worst of mud and dust is walked off before the main carpets are reached. Use in porches as well as inside front and back doors.

Dusting: Start from the higher surfaces and work down-wards. An old-fashioned feather duster or its modern synthe-tic equivalent is useful for light fittings and high shelves. Dust after vacuuming.

Vacuuming: Finish work upstairs, then leave the cleaner tucked away on the landing, ready to start vacuuming upstairs the next time. Next time, leave it downstairs and work in the opposite order. This saves carrying it around needlessly.

Food mixers: Mixers, processors and other kitchen equip-ment can be quickly cleaned of food splashes and greasy marks with cream cleanser on a damp cloth.

Multipurpose spray cleaner: Cleaner that can be used on wood, glass and plastic is a real timesaver, as almost all the hard surfaces in a room can be polished at once.

Rubber gloves: For any really filthy work or for when you are handling water, wear a good strong pair of rubber gloves. If you find them difficult to get on, then dust the inside with a little talcum powder. To dry them, stretch them over an empty milk bottle. This will prevent them from perishing, which they will do if they are left wet.

Feather duster: Check over the paintwork and picture rail, and remove the dust with a cloth or feather duster.

Polishing mit: Make a polishing mit from an old woollen sock. Wear like a glove when polishing.

Saucepans: Pans are easier to clean if they are filled with warm water and a little washing-up liquid as soon as they are emptied. Very dirty pans can be soaked overnight in a little biological washing powder. Wash and rinse, then boil up some fresh water to remove all traces of detergent.

Sheets: Once sheets are completely dry they are hard to iron. If you have an electric blanket, put the sheets on the bed creased, and turn the blanket on for about half an hour. This will get rid of all the creases with little effort. Only do this with a completely dry sheet, and cover it with the quilt or blankets to keep the warmth in. Alternatively, fold and stack the sheets in a pile in the airing cupboard.

Remove cushions: Sofas and chairs collect all sorts of dust and dirt. Remember to remove cushions and vacuum underneath regularly to extend the life of the chairs.

Tablecloths: Linen cloths look good but do need a lot of washing and ironing. For family use, a thick PVC tablecloth makes a practical alternative as it can be wiped over after each meal. PVC can be bought by the yard and is available in a wide range of designs. Cut to shape using pinking shears.

Washing up: Washing up that cannot be tackled at once is best stacked in a bowl of warm water, with a little washing-up liquid added. This prevents food particles drying on.

Wastepaper bins: Line bins with a circle of wallpaper or folded newspaper to make them quick to empty.

Pockets: Wear an apron with large pockets when cleaning, so that all the odds and ends you discover as you go around the house can be picked up to be sorted out later.

Household cleaners

The following alphabetical list gives details of cleaning liquids and powders (see also 'Stain Removal' page 140). Some are proprietary solutions and some are household storecupboard items which have a secondary function as cleaners.

AEROSOL CLEANERS

These are generally multipurpose cleaners and polishers that can be used on glass, mirrors, wood, plastic and many other hard surfaces.

BICARBONATE OF SODA

Mix 1 teaspoon of bicarbonate with 300 ml ($\frac{1}{2}$ pint) of warm water for a good mild cleaner, that will not leave any lingering smells. It's ideal for the inside of fridges and freezers and for plastic food storage boxes.

Use neat on a damp cloth for stubborn marks and stains on worktops, plastics and household equipment.

BLEACH

Dilute this as directed on the container as strengths vary. Use for cleaning WC pans, drains and sinks. It is also useful on paths and any area that has had mould or mildew growing on it. Use diluted (as directed) on large areas or half and half with water on small areas of hard surfaces.

Never mix bleach with other household cleaners as toxic fumes may be given off.

BORAX

Use 1 tablespoon to 600 ml (1 pint) of warm water. This has a mild bleaching effect and is useful for removing acid-based stains. Soak fabrics for ten minutes or so, then remove to prevent the fabric becoming bleached. Always do a test piece before use.

CREAM CLEANSERS

These are good general purpose cleaners. The creamy texture prevents scratching on baths, basins and other hard surfaces and they are easy to use neat on small areas of paintwork and worktops as well. Look for the VEDC (Vitreous Enamel Development Council) sign on cream cleansers, which shows they are suitable for vitreous enamel.

GREASE SOLVENTS

These are available in aerosol and liquid form. Follow the instructions on the container. They are useful to have on hand as many stains are grease-based. They can also be used for removing any residual colour left after the main stain has been removed. Avoid inhaling the fumes. Store safely.

HOUSEHOLD SODA

This is sold in powder form and can be mixed with water to clean any greasy areas. Follow the instructions on the packet. It is very effective for sinks and drains. As it is quite strong, do not tackle delicate items or areas and do not use to clean aluminium pans, as it can cause pitting.

LIQUID CLEANERS

Generally these are quite concentrated detergents that can be used neat or diluted. They are effective for removing greasy dirt, and some spray types are available which make cleaning inaccessible areas easier. Follow the directions on the container.

METHYLATED SPIRIT

Use neat on a white cloth, or for small areas apply on a cotton bud. This is a good general purpose solvent for cleaning and stain removal but always check that the fibre will not be affected, by doing a test first. It is highly flammable, so extinguish any naked flames and work in a well ventilated area. Store safely in a locked cupboard.

POLISHES

Liquid polishes are usually enriched, therefore are good for natural woods and other porous surfaces. Apply sparingly and rub in well. Paste polishes require a fair bit of elbow grease to produce a shine.

VINEGAR

To make a *weak solution* use 1 teaspoon to 300 ml ($\frac{1}{2}$ pint) of water. For a *strong solution*, use twice this much vinegar to water. It is good for removing a light film of grease and for washing hard surfaces. On bathroom tiles in hard water areas, it can be used to remove the hard water stains that sometimes appear. Use half vinegar and half water for this purpose. Prevent stains from building up by rinsing tiles regularly with a weak vinegar solution.

WASHING-UP LIQUID

Use this when hot soapy water is required. Apart from general washing up it is also useful for cleaning paintwork and other hard surfaces. It can also be used for removing stains from upholstery and carpets by mixing 1–2 teaspoons with a cup of warm water and apply the foam only.

Note
Never mix different types of strong household cleaners, and do not use them in quantity with the windows closed. The fumes given off can be dangerous even when used on their own.

79

Cleaning room by room

BATHROOMS

Bathmats: Sealed cork bathmats just need to be wiped with a damp cloth. If they are unsealed cork, seal them yourself, otherwise wipe with a damp cloth. Small plastic mats can be washed in the sink in soapy water but large ones will need to be cleaned outside with soapy water and a stiff brush. Fabric bathmats can usually be washed: follow the care label instructions.

Vitreous enamel baths: Baths made from vitreous enamel can be cleaned with a good cream cleanser. Avoid harsh powder cleaners, as they cause fine scratching on the surface. In hard water areas there is often a build-up of hard water deposits around the plughole, the overflow and the taps. Dripping taps can also stain the bath. There are proprietary cleaners that will remove these stains, available from hardware shops, but do use and store these with care, as they are very strong solutions. Follow the manufacturer's instructions carefully and store them out of the reach of children. If these stains are not too ingrained, try dipping a cut lemon in salt and working this into the stained area, leave to stand for a couple of minutes, then rinse well. Do not leave for longer, as the acidic effects may damage the enamel. Repeat this procedure if necessary several times, rinsing well in between.

Deposits around taps can be cleaned with an old toothbrush dipped in cream cleanser.

Plastic or acrylic baths: Baths and basins made from plastic or acrylic have been introduced over recent years and these need a different cleaning system. For day-to-day cleaning

80

wipe with washing-up liquid on a cloth. Resistant stains can be rubbed with half a lemon, then rinsed well. Light scratches and dull areas can be improved with a little silver polish. Rub in, then buff up.

Bidets: Bidets are made of ceramic. Wipe daily with a mild detergent or soapy solution. Use this treatment on the taps as well. More stubborn marks can be removed with a smooth cream cleaner. Never use a powder cleaner on ceramic ware as it is abrasive and may damage the surface.

Flooring: Treat flooring according to type. Sealed cork tiles, vinyl and lino can all be mopped lightly with floor cleaner. Waxed cork tiles and wood floors need a liquid solvent-based polish. Recently, special carpeting for bathrooms and kitchens has been introduced. To look after it, follow the instructions supplied with the carpet. Avoid putting natural jute-backed carpet in the bathroom as the backing can be affected by damp.

Light fittings: When dusting light fittings, make sure the fitment is switched off and the bulb is cool. Remove with dry hands, dust and, if necessary, wipe with a well wrung out cloth. Wipe dry and replace the bulb. Dust around the fitting, with a feather duster or dusting cloth. Murphy's Law dictates that the more difficult the light fitting is to reach, the more often the bulb will need replacing, so while cleaning the fitment, it may well be worth replacing the light bulb to save trouble later.

Mirrors: Clean mirrors with a damp cloth and a little washing-up liquid, or any good window cleaner. Remove hairspray with methylated spirit on cotton wool. Prevent steaming up by rubbing with a little neat washing-up liquid, or use an antimisting product.

Potplants: While spring cleaning the bathroom remove all the plants to the kitchen sink and stand them in an inch or so of water. Clean dust from the leaves with a damp cloth or use a leafshine product and check if any plants need repotting.

Paintwork: Wash down using washing-up liquid and warm water. Do not use washing powders as these may affect the appearance of the paintwork. Dust picture rails, ledges and door panelling before washing, to prevent the dust sticking to the wet woodwork. Very dirty paintwork can be washed with a weak sugar soap solution, available from DIY stores.

Dirty walls: On really dirty walls, work from the bottom upwards to avoid streaky lines running through the dirt, as these are very difficult to remove. Use two buckets, one with soapy water and one with rinsing water. Wet the cloth or sponge in the soapy water, clean a small area, then rinse the cloth in the other bucket. Repeat on the next small area. This avoids putting dirt back on the wall. Rinse, following the same procedure.

Shower curtains: If your shower curtains develop dark spots of mildew, wash with a mild bleach or antiseptic solution, using 2 teaspoons of solution to ½litre (1 pint) water, and wipe dry. Avoid this problem by pulling the curtain across after use to allow air to circulate and dry the curtain.

Shower heads: Modern plastic shower heads can often be removed and taken to pieces. Ensure both water and power are turned off first, then remove the shower head and wash the plastic rings in warm water and vinegar: use about one tablespoon of vinegar to ½litre (1 pint) water. For a build-up of hard water deposit on chrome showerheads use a cut lemon, as described on page 80. Scrub the pieces with an old toothbrush to remove hard water deposits, which sometimes slow down the water flow. Dry the pieces and put them back together again.

Shower trays: Wipe shower trays daily with a mild detergent or warm soapy water. For stubborn marks use a very smooth cream cleaner.

Sponges: Real sponges sometimes become quite slimy. Wash them in a weak vinegar solution (see page 79) and allow them to dry naturally, outside if possible.

Tiles: Wipe tiles over with a cream cleanser and a damp cloth, then rinse off. In hard water areas, tiles often show water splashes even when completely clean. This is particularly noticeable on dark shiny colours. Rinse the tiles with warm water and vinegar, in equal amounts, then wipe dry and buff up.

Washbasins: Wipe down washbasins daily with a mild soap solution, rinse and dry. Use the same soap solution on the taps. Stronger cleaners should be used only if necessary and then only sparingly. Never use abrasive powder cleaners which may damage the surface.

WC pans: Clean the WC pan with a soft brush and a recommended cleanser. Pay particular attention to cleaning under the rim. Don't use harsh cleansers which may damage the glaze. Wash the seat, handle or chain and surrounding areas with warm soapy water and disinfectant. Wash the toilet brush in hot water and disinfectant.

BEDROOMS

Bedheads: Upholstered bedheads can generally be vacuumed and shampooed with upholstery shampoo. Brass bedsteads can be cleaned with a brass cleaner. If very tarnished, clean with a lemon dipped in salt. Cane bedheads can be cleaned with a general purpose spray cleaner.

Beds: It is worthwhile pushing the vacuum cleaner attachment under the bed whenever possible to remove dust before it builds up. With beds that have storage drawers or that come down to the floor this is not possible, and indeed it seems illogical that dust can collect underneath but it does, so move the bed out once a year and clean underneath.

Blankets: If blankets will fit in the washing machine, the job is much easier. If they will not, consider taking them to the local launderette, where the washing machines are usually larger. Hand washing usually has to be done in the bath; soak first in cold water, then wash in warm soapy water. (See page 145.) If machine washing, use a wool programme with a very short spin as many blankets will lose their shape if spun for long periods. Check the washcare label on any blanket before treating. Dry cleaning is another option, but do not use coin-operated dry cleaning machines as the fumes remaining in the blanket are noxious. Send to a specialist cleaner instead.

Duvets: Duvets with synthetic fillings can be washed, by hand or by machine. Feather and down-filled duvets cannot be washed and need to be sent to a specialist cleaner. In either case the filling is not improved by cleaning and it is best to avoid if possible. Instead use a cover, and deal with any spills and splashes as quickly as possible. Push the filling away from the affected area, hold it back with a large elastic band and treat the outer case.

Mattresses: On old beds, where the springs are not enclosed, stains sometimes appear on the underside of the mattress, so an old blanket, or even a layer of thick paper between the springs and the mattress is a good idea.

Pillows: Avoid washing pillows if at all possible as they take so long to dry. (See page 145.) Tackle stains promptly by spot treating. Never put pillows into a tumble drier because of their weight and do not use a coin-operated dry cleaning machine for fear of toxic fumes which can sometimes remain in the filling.

Pillow coverings: If the covering to a pillow is badly damaged, either fit a new cover on top, or tack the new cover on to the end of the old one. Sew almost all the way round, then cut the end of the old cover, so that the filling can simply be shaken into the new case. Unpick the tacking and sew up the remaining seam neatly.

GENERAL ROOMS

A face lift for carpets: If spring sunshine gleaming on the carpet makes it look dull, try vacuuming first, then wring a cloth out in vinegar and warm water and wipe the carpet over with this. Sometimes this will remove a fine greasy layer on the carpet and brighten the colours.

Shampooing carpets: When shampooing is necessary, do a test patch first to make sure that the dye will not run. Apply a little foam shampoo on a hidden corner, work in with a brush and cover with a piece of white cloth. If the cloth picks up the colour of the carpet, abandon plans to shampoo it and either learn to love it as it is or call in a professional. If not, go ahead and use a foam shampoo. Spread it thinly and evenly over the carpet with a mop. Allow to dry, then vacuum off. Beware of over-wetting the carpet, which will cause shrinkage and protect the legs of furniture with little 'socks' made of cling film or paper. Treat existing stains before shampooing.

Cleaning carpets and upholstery: Hot water extraction cleaning, sometimes incorrectly described as steam cleaning, is another alternative, both for carpets and upholstery. This can be done by a company or the cleaner can be hired by the day or week. It is often worthwhile teaming up with several friends to hire one for a week and share the cost. The only problem is that they generally work so well you decide to clean the whole house and end up still cleaning at midnight because your neighbour is using it the next day!

They are quite large heavy machines into which you put water and a cleaning agent. You then use them rather like a vacuum cleaner. They spray the hot water into the carpet, then suck it, and an amazing amount of dirt, out. You need a fine day, as there seems to be a great deal of moisture around, so doors and windows need to be opened. Keep the nozzle moving evenly and steadily. Beware of overwetting your carpets!

Calling in the professionals: Make sure any carpet cleaning firm you call in is a member of the Carpet Cleaners Association; the CCA ensures that customers can trust its members to carry out cleaning to a high standard and to provide fair trading practices.

Vacuuming curtains: Almost all curtains benefit from occasional vacuuming to remove dust. Use the dusting attachment and concentrate on the folds at the top. If possible, take the curtains down and remove the hooks or rings. Unpleat the tops by pulling the tapes through (provided you have not cut the ends off), then air for an hour or so out on the line. This will help remove dust as well.

Glass fibre curtains: It is possible to wash glass fibre curtains if you are careful. Wash them in a bath of warm soapy water, taking care not to fold or crush them. Wear rubber gloves as the little fibres can irritate the skin. Rinse well and lay them over parallel lines without folding, or put a few plastic hooks back in the tapes and hang by these on a line. Rehang at the window while still slightly damp and pull gently into shape. Do not iron.

In the wash: Many types of curtains can be washed by hand or machine. Many fabrics shrink when washed, so allowance should be made for this when buying curtains. Take the hem down before washing to aid removal of the hemline. Mark hook positions with nail varnish before washing. For hand washing, soak the curtains first in cold water to remove dust and dirt, when wash in warm soapy water, rinse well and hang out to dry.

Hooks and tracks: Wash plastic hooks and wipe plastic curtain tracks using warm soapy water. Dry, then polish with a silicone polish to encourage the curtains to pull smoothly. Rub metal tracks lightly with a little metal polish.

Special care: Very large curtains and curtains made from cotton velvet, and other pile fabrics, wools, and some man-made fabrics should all be dry-cleaned.

Renovating floorboards: Floorboards with an old seal can be renovated. Use a fine grade steel wool dipped in white spirit. Keep a window open and ensure any naked flames are extinguished. Work in small areas, mopping as you go. Allow to dry before applying a new coat of seal. Do not use wire wool on hardwood as it may cause iron staining.

Wood furniture: Natural wood needs regular dusting and polishing with furniture polish to keep it in good condition. Old stripped wood generally benefits from a light application of good wax polish or cabinet makers' polish. Finger marks on waxed furniture can be removed by wiping with a cloth wrung out in a mixture of 2 tablespoons of vinegar to $\frac{1}{2}$litre (1 pint) of warm water. French polished wood can simply be cleaned with a spray polish.

Plastic furniture: Plastic furniture can be wiped with a damp cloth and often cleaned with a general purpose spray.

Radiators: Try cleaning behind radiators by padding the end of a garden bamboo cane, then tying an old sock over this. You should be able to reach the difficult parts with this.

Leather upholstery: Leather sofas and chairs can be kept supple by using the recommended polish occasionally. Some have special finishes, so keep and follow the makers' instructions.

Cleaning chairs: All sofas and chairs benefit from occasional vacuuming or thorough brushing. Remove all cushions and clean underneath, then vacuum and brush the arms and back

87

of the sofa. Dust and dirt can penetrate the fibres and eventually rot them, so this regular cleaning is well worth while. Most fabrics can be shampooed, although some such as cotton velvet, chenilles, tapestry, silk and wool are best left to the professionals.

Sofa coverings: Acrylic velvet and many other sofa coverings can be cleaned using the foam only from upholstery shampoo. This is available in a liquid form that needs mixing with water, or in an aerosol can with a brush attachment. It makes the whole job much easier and is worth the extra expense. Treat any existing stains first, and always do a spot check on a small piece of the fabric at the back. Apply the foam, on a small brush or using the can, wipe it over the fabric, allow to dry thoroughly, then vacuum off.

Loose covers: Loose covers can be removed and washed or cleaned as appropriate. If washing, replace them while still just damp to make sure they fit well.

KITCHEN

Cupboards: Modern plastic shelves in cupboards simply need wiping with a cream cleanser. However, larder cupboards and old-fashioned wooden shelving need to be washed with warm soapy water and a small brush. Dry well and line the shelves with several layers of wallpaper. This means that once one layer is dirty, you can simply remove it leaving the clean layer underneath, ready for use. Don't use ready pasted vinyls though, as they tend to stick together and the pasted backing should not be used anywhere near food.

Tins and jars: While sorting cupboards, wipe the base of tins and jars to prevent them marking the shelves.

Breadbins: Wipe round breadbins every week or so. Use a little warm water and vinegar, and dry well before replacing the bread. If left-over bread has become mouldy, wipe and dry the bin before use. Stand the bin outside in the sunshine to dry it and get rid of any lingering mould.

Equipment: All the major appliances like cookers, fridges, washing machines need really to be pulled out away from the wall so that the floor behind them may be cleaned. Rollers are fitted on many appliances and can be bought separately for others, and, of course, these make life much easier. Beware of dragging heavy equipment across vinyl floors as this will damage them. The outside of appliances can be cleaned with a cream cleanser. Small scratches can be rubbed down, then covered with white appliance paint available from hardware shops. For cleaning the inside of various appliances, see the section on equipment.

Extractor fans: Extractor fans often become quite greasy during use. Switch off the fan and unplug before cleaning. If there is no separate plug, remove the fuse from the spur socket or turn off at the mains. Then remove the outer cover, which can be washed in warm soapy water. The fan blades should be wiped with a just damp cloth. Do not wet this area. Replace the cover after drying. The outside grid, which is also usually removable, can be washed in warm soapy water and dried before replacing. Clean regularly to prevent a build-up of grease. Once a year should be enough in most households.

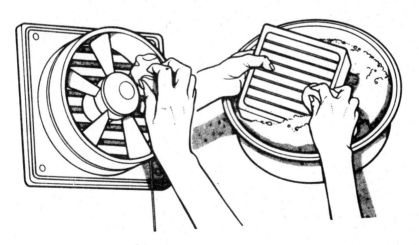

Floor care: Sealed wooden floors, sealed cork tiles, lino, thermo-plastic tiles and vinyl flooring can all be damp mopped daily to keep them looking good. Use water sparingly on all of these surfaces.

The seal on wooden floors often wears unevenly, so needs removing and resealing. To do this, use fine grade steel wool dipped in white spirit and rub over the floor surface. Work in small areas, mopping up as you go. Make sure there are no naked lights (check gas fires and boilers) and work with a window or door open. Once all the remaining seal has been removed, very lightly mop the floor and allow to dry well before applying a new polyurethane seal.

Carpet tiles: Carpet tiles can be vacuumed and individual tiles can be lifted and replaced or shampooed with carpet shampoo to remove stains and soiling.

Ceramic tiles: Glazed ceramic tiles can be washed with hot soapy water, then rinsed. Stubborn marks can be cleaned with a liquid household cleaner, or a damp cloth.

Built up polish: Fixed floor tiles that have been constantly polished with a self-shining polish often become rather cloudy around the edges of the room. This is because of a build-up of polish. To remove this use 2 tablespoons of powder floor cleaner to half a bucket of cold water. Add about a cup of household ammonia. Wash the floor with this mixture. Mop up and dry well before polishing sparingly with a self-shining polish.

Regular defrost: Defrost the refrigerator, ideally, once a week before you do the main shopping trip. Speed up the process by filling the ice-tray with boiling water and putting it back in the ice-making compartment. Do not use detergent inside: wash the refrigerator inside and out with a solution of borax in hot water, including the shelves. Rinse with fresh water and blot dry with a piece of old clean towelling before you switch on again. A solution of bicarbonate of soda can also be used, instead of the borax. Use a handful of bicarbonate to a bowl of water.

Sinks: Sinks can be cleaned with a cream cleanser, or filled with hot water and a little bleach. Stainless steel sinks benefit from the occasional spring clean with stainless steel cleaner, but on a day-to-day basis, cream cleanser will do the trick. Occasionally put a handful of household soda in the sink and run the hot tap for a minute or two to clean the waste and pipes of grease. Overflows can be cleaned with a small toothbrush or bottle brush, but make sure your clothes are covered, as both tend to splash greasy particles at you.

Cleaning the slats: Venetian blinds can be cleaned by soaking a pair of fabric gloves in soapy water, putting them on and sliding each slat between the fingers.

Taps: Clean taps with warm soapy water or a mild cream cleanser. Hard water deposits around the tap base can be tackled with a little cream cleanser on an old toothbrush, or mix in a little lemon juice and salt and apply on a toothbrush. Rub in well, leave for a couple of minutes, then rinse off thoroughly. (Do not leave for longer, as the acid may damage the chrome.) Hard water deposits around the spout of a tap may be treated with half a lemon. Cover the bath or sink with an old towel as the lemon juice might bleach it, then push the cut surface of the lemon on to the tap spout and work round. If this system does not work, try a water softener. This is usually sold in powder form at chemists, and is then mixed with water, using 2 teaspoons to ½litre (1 pint).

Hard water build-up: If there is a build-up of hard water deposits, hang a plastic container full of water softener and water around the tap, so that the outlet is immersed in the mixture. Leave for about two hours, then repeat the process if necessary.

Worktops: Work surfaces are mostly laminates and are best cleaned with cream cleansers, or with a little dry bicarbonate of soda on a damp cloth. Wipe up spills as they occur and protect the surface from hot pans and dishes. Avoid cutting on laminate worktops as this will damage the surface and may make them difficult to clean.

When all
else fails

Never panic: Panic usually sets in when the cooking is not going as rapidly as planned, the children are restless and you are expecting guests in ten minutes, one hour or that evening and the house is a total mess. The golden rule here has to be not to try to clean and tidy everywhere. Far better to do the absolute minimum, then concentrate on distracting and entertaining your guests. With a little luck this will work so well that they will not have time to notice the dust, or sticky fingermarks on the doors.

Quick move: If you have no time for vacuuming, move a rug around since it is likely to be clean underneath, and add a couple of floor cushions.

Thoughtful touches: Cheer up a spare bedroom with flowers, or a pot plant from another room, a carafe of water and a few books and magazines. These touches will demonstrate that you care about your guests' comfort and they will be far less likely to notice the dust, or dirty windows.

Instant tidy: Collect all the odds and ends that make a room look untidy. Load them on to a tray and hide this in the bedroom.

Collections: Collections usually impress people and make a topic of conversation. Make lots of odds and ends look like a collection by linking them together; fill odd containers such as glasses, boxes, jars, little trays, sea shells, shallow dishes, and so on with miniature soaps, tiny sweets or fabric flowers. Group together on a shelf or table to make a focal point.

Keep guests busy: Offer drinks, be it tea or gin-and-tonics as soon as possible, and supply biscuits or other nibbles as well. Stay with them if at all possible; left alone they will have time to inspect the room!

Open fires: It is worth the effort to light an open fire, even if it is not really cold enough to need it. If you can borrow a cat to curl up in front of it, so much the better!

Cover up: Plants and flowers cover up an amazing amount of untidiness. Borrow them from the bathroom and bedroom if necessary. Position them in groups for best effect and use them to cover up the odd tear in the wallpaper or stain on the carpet, if necessary.

Smells: Cover unwelcome smells with pot pourri, incense, perfumed candles or, if desperate, air freshener. Create pleasant smells by making fresh coffee, warming a loaf of bread in the oven or burning a few herbs, such as rosemary, under the grill.

Sofas: Sofas often become quite tatty, and oddly enough you never notice until other people are coming. Make your sofa instantly prettier by collecting all the small cushions in the house and arranging them on it. Alternatively, throw an ethnic style bedspread or even a length of spare curtain fabric over it.

Bathroom welcome: Put out fresh towels and pretty soaps in the bathroom. Wash round the hand basin and spray a little air freshener around.

Instant curtains: Windows without curtains look bleak. If you are entertaining in a new house, make instant curtains from sheets, or yards of fabric. Wrap these around the curtain pole or track, and swag back with brightly-coloured ribbon or even shoe laces. Alternatively, line the windowledge with an attractive display of empty glass bottles, so the light shines through them. Avoid gin bottles though if you want to create a good impression with Great Aunt Ethel!

93

A-Z of general cleaning

BAMBOO

Dust or vacuum regularly. Wash occasionally using warm soapy water plus a little borax or salt. Dip a soft brush in this and scrub the bamboo lightly. Rinse well with salty water and allow to dry naturally. Occasional polishing with a linseed oil will keep the bamboo supple and help prevent splitting.

CANE AND WICKER

Clean regularly with a spray cleaner. Varnished cane can simply be wiped over occasionally with a damp cloth. Unvarnished cane can be washed with warm water and washing soda mixture. Bleach stains with weak household bleach solution. See also page 197 for details on tightening up a stretched cane seat.

If cane is beyond cleaning, consider painting. Use a spray paint of the type sold for cars. This makes it easy to apply and gives a wide range of colours, including gold, or glossy black which looks good on cane.

CARPETS

Vacuum regularly to prevent dust and grit working its way deep into the pile. When a carpet is laid, save a spare piece to use for testing stain removers on. It's essential to know what can be safely used on each carpet in the house, so you can act quickly if necessary. Before using *any* cleaning agent or stain removal treatment on carpets you should do a test piece first on a spare piece or on a hidden area. (See stain removal pages 140–176).

CERAMIC HOBS

These can be cleaned with a specialist cleaner and this should be done regularly to keep the finish in good condition. Stains sometimes respond to a paste of the cleaner. Mix the cleaner with a little water, then spread over the area and leave it to dry. Rinse and dry well afterwards.

CHROME

A little paraffin applied on a clean cloth will restore the shine to chrome. Alternatively, use a general purpose spray cleaner or chrome cleaner sold in car accessory shops.

CORK TILES

Floor tiles are usually sealed with a polyurethane seal or waxed. Sealed tiles need only light mopping and can then be polished with a water-based polish. Waxed cork should not be washed but cleaned with a solvent-based polish. Cork wall tiles are not usually sealed, but can be rather dusty. Brush lightly and treat stains with a damp cloth.

DRAWERS

A musty smell in unused drawers can often be removed by filling the drawer with screwed-up newspaper and leaving it slightly ajar for a day or two, or, if possible, leave the drawer outside in the sunshine for a while. Another way of dealing with the mustiness is to put some lemon peel in the drawer. To keep a drawer smelling sweet, use perfumed drawer liners.

GLASS

Glass shelves and coffee tables can be cleaned by wiping with a mixture of vinegar and water, or use a window cleaner or general purpose spray cleaner. Fine scratches can be removed using a metal polish on wadding. Rub round in small circles and rinse off.

KETTLES

In hard water areas use a defurring solution regularly, as a thick build-up of hard water deposits will slow down an electric kettle and increase running costs. Vinegar is a good alternative to defurring agents. Cover the element with vinegar, bring just to the boil, then turn off and allow to cool. Empty and rinse several times. Boil the kettle at least once and empty the water away before use. Defurring solutions are stronger, so use with care.

LEATHER

Leather furniture generally needs little daily care, although occasional treating with the recommended polish, used sparingly, will help keep it supple.

Dirty marks on leather luggage can be removed with a damp cloth. On old luggage that has become rather battered, use water with a little vinegar and add just a dash of ammonia to it, then wipe over the leather with a damp cloth. Finish with an enriched furniture cream.

LINOLEUM

The pattern on lino is often printed on the surface and strong detergents will eventually take this printing off. Therefore, occasional mopping with warm water and washing-up liquid should be the regular cleaning method. Occasional polishing with a solvent-based polish will keep the flooring in good condition.

MARBLE

On a day-to-day basis marble simply needs wiping with a damp soapy cloth. As it is porous, it does stain easily. Using half a lemon on stains will fade them but great care must be taken to prevent the acid affecting the marble. It is best to leave the lemon for just a couple of minutes, then rinse the area well and repeat the procedure several times, so that the marble can be checked for signs of any damage.

SAUCEPANS

Wash aluminium pans in hot soapy water. Burnt-on foods can be soaked off, or use a saucepan brush and an abrasive powder. Black stains in hard water areas are harmless but they can be removed by boiling up lemon skins or apple peelings for about 15 minutes. To prevent a black stain appearing, add a slice of lemon to the water when steaming or pressure cooking.

Nonstick finishes generally only need washing in hot soapy water. For old pans, boil a little warm water and washing-up liquid in the pan, then brush well with a saucepan brush or nonstick cleaning pad. (See also page 184.)

SILVER

There are a wide range of silver cleaners on the market, including a dip that is very useful for small, intricate pieces of silverware. Protect your hands by wearing rubber gloves.

Silver can also be cleaned by immersing it in a bowl containing a handful of washing soda and a handful of milk bottle tops. Add sufficient hot water to cover the silver. The tarnish is removed and collects on the milk bottle tops, but it may also collect on any silver protruding from the water, so ensure it is all submerged. Fumes may be given off by this process, so work with the window open. Once the mixture stops fizzing or as soon as the silver is clean, remove it and buff up with a soft cloth. An impregnated silver cloth is useful either to shine up silver quickly, or to wrap around silver that is to be stored. These can be bought or you can make your own. Use 10 parts cold water, 2 parts ammonia and 1 part long-term silver polish. Soak some squares of cotton in this, then leave them to drip dry.

SLATE

General cleaning simply involves washing or scrubbing with hot soapy water. Dull slate can be brightened up by mixing equal quantities of linseed oil and white spirit. Apply this on a soft cloth and buff up well.

STONE

This can be cleaned by scrubbing with plain water, or specialist cleaners are available. If you have trouble tracking these down, try your local builders' merchant.

VACUUM FLASKS

These often become quite musty in storage. After use, rinse well and drain. Store with the lid off. Use a tea or coffee stain remover, available from chemists, or half fill with warm water and add a little bicarbonate of soda (about 2 teaspoons). Put the lid on and shake well. Soak overnight if necessary.

VENETIAN BLINDS

These need regular dusting either with a special blind cleaning tool or with an old cotton glove. Put the glove on and run your hand along the slats. Very dirty blinds can be washed in the bath. Protect the bath with an old towel and wash the blinds in a little warm soapy water, taking care to keep the mechanism out of the water. If the blinds are too big for the bath, there are specialist steam cleaning companies around who will do the job for you.

VINYL FLOORING

This generally needs only light mopping. Do not overwet and work in circles. Scratch marks can be improved slightly by using a little metal polish on a cloth.

WALLPAPER

An international set of symbols is now being used in wallpaper pattern books and on product labels. It includes symbols on wallpaper care, and these should be followed when treating marks. Use a spray dry cleaner for greasy marks, but remember to do a test area first. Other marks may respond to a soft, clean artist's rubber.

Washable wallpapers are really only spongeable; use a sponge dipped in warm water with a little washing-up liquid. Squeeze the sponge well, so that it is damp rather than wet, then wipe over the wallpaper.

Vinyls are tougher; even crayon marks can be removed with a damp cloth. This makes them an ideal choice for children's rooms.

Hessian and similar wallcoverings cannot be washed. Instead, vacuum them with the vacuum cleaner dusting attachment.

WOOD

Floorboards can be scrubbed with hot soapy water as long as they are mopped up well. Do not make the wood too wet as too much moisture will cause the wood to swell and the floorboards to buckle. Sealed wooden floors simply need light mopping and can be buffed up with a duster tied to a broom or with a special cotton mop.

Most furniture can be cleaned with a spray polish. French polished wood generally needs only dusting and occasional polishing with a good wax polish. Remove sticky marks and a build-up of wax by wiping over with a cloth dipped in warm water and just a little vinegar. A chamois leather gives the best results. Buff up when dry.

Most modern furniture is veneered and this simply needs regular dusting and occasional polishing with a spray polish. Some modern woods have special finishes (such as a plasticized finish), so always check with the maker's instructions before cleaning or removing stains. Always do a test piece, when tackling stains and marks on any furniture.

Removing unwanted smells

CIGARETTE SMOKE

Lavender oil: A mixture of household soda, a few drops of ammonia and some lavender oil infused with boiling water should get rid of stale tobacco smells. If the smell persists, dilute a few drops of ammonia in some water and leave in the room overnight.

Absorbing vinegar: A small bowl of vinegar placed in the room while people are smoking will absorb the smell of the smoke.

In a damp spin: To get rid of lingering smoke spin a damp towel around the room.

COOKING AND KITCHEN SMELLS

Lovely lemon: When cooking cabbage, put a little fresh lemon juice in the water with it – this will stop the cooking smells from spreading, without affecting the taste of the vegetable. Or, add a slice of stale bread, it takes away the smell and can be skimmed off the surface easily afterwards.

On the board: Chopping boards tend to absorb the smell of foods. These can be difficult to get rid of by washing. Rub a paste of bicarbonate of soda into the board, rinse and wash as usual.

Salt removes onion smell: To eradicate the smell of onion from a wooden chopping board, rub it over with coarse salt then rinse with cold water.

100

Boiling white vinegar: Smells will disappear from a saucepan if you boil a little white vinegar in it.

Absorbing thought: If you are cooking something with a smell that you do not want to travel all over the house keep a saucer of vinegar at your side. It will absorb most of the smell.

Into the fire: Coffee grounds can be used to get rid of unpleasant odours in rooms. Boil some up in a saucepan, or throw some into an open fire.

Onion and garlic on hands: When you have onion or garlic smells on your hands, the trick is to wash them as quickly as possible in cold water. Hot water seals the smell into the skin. If the smell persists, rub your hands with lemon juice or vinegar and wash with soap and water.

Bleach out: Vinegar will remove the smell left when you have been washing with diluted bleach. Just rub a little over your hands.

Fishy thoughts 1: If silver cutlery has a fishy smell clinging to it, add a drop of mustard to the washing-up water. A little vinegar added to the water will remove fish smells from china.

Fishy thoughts 2: To get rid of the smell of fish from a frying pan put salt in it and add boiling water then leave to soak.

Fishy thoughts 3: A few pieces of celery dropped into the cooking oil will help to disguise the smell of fried fish.

Garlic on breath: Chew a piece of fresh parsley or, if you can bear it, a coffee bean, to relieve garlicky breath.

PETS

Litter tray: Make sure that used litter is removed daily and use an air freshener.

101

Accidents: If your cat or dog has been sick on a carpet, a quick squirt from the soda syphon will help to get rid of the smell, once you have cleared up.

REFRIGERATOR

Stubborn smells: Smells very often linger in the refrigerator and are difficult to get rid of. They can be absorbed by one of these substances: charcoal, cat litter, baking soda, or crumpled newspaper. A small amount of any of these should absorb smells. If the smell persists then wipe the inside of the refrigerator with a solution of sterilizing fluid used for babies' bottles. Do not use on metal. Rinse the inside of the refrigerator and leave to dry before you switch it on again.

Make a paste: A paste of baking soda smeared around the inside of the refrigerator will also get rid of lingering odours.

SHOES

Baking soda: A little baking soda in shoes will absorb any smells. Sprinkle it into the shoes and leave overnight before removing.

CUPBOARDS

Bath salts: Put a saucer full of bath salts on the floor of a little-used cupboard. It will keep clothes fresh and dispel musty smells.

Charcoal: Activated charcoal will eat up musty smells in small cupboards.

BATHROOM

Strike a match: Unwanted smells in the bathroom will disappear if you strike a match and let it burn down. Do not leave the room until you are sure the match has gone out.

102

GLOVES

Lavender for gloves: Keep gloves smelling fresh by putting a lavender sachet in the drawer with them.

NEW PAINT AND CHEMICALS

A bowl of salt: Leave a small bowl of salt in a newly painted room overnight. This will get rid of paint smells.

Onion and water: A peeled onion in a bucket of water will remove very strong chemical smells.

DUSTBINS

Fly off: Putting mothballs in the bottom of a dustbin will make it smell better and deter flies.

NICE SMELLS

Oranges and lemons: If you have an open fire, throw orange and lemon peel on to it. The room will soon be filled with a very pleasant smell.

Household pests

GENERAL PREVENTION

Many of the pests listed below are attracted to our houses in search of warmth and food. So with this in mind there are several things you can do to prevent pests from bothering you in your general housekeeping.

1. Make sure that you wipe up food crumbs thoroughly after each meal.
2. Make sure that pet food is taken up once the pet has finished with it, so that flies do not lay their eggs in it.
3. Make sure that your dustbin is always covered with a lid, otherwise you will find that flies will use it as a breeding ground.
4. Regularly clean the drains out and make sure that they are not blocked.

SAFE PROCEDURES WITH PEST REPELLANTS

Read and heed: There are many proprietary products on the market which deal with most sorts of pests but it is essential to follow a few safety rules. Read the manufacturer's instructions and cautions fully.

Poisonous waste: If you have some of the poison left over then make sure that you either put it back into the correct container or that you dispose of it safely. Many liquid products can be flushed down the drains, but follow this with copious amounts of water to ensure that it gets right down the system.

104

Wash your hands of it: Always be careful when handling the products. If you do splash your skin, then wash off immediately. Wash your hands well after you have been using the poison.

Careful spraying: Aerosol treatment should only be used in a well-ventilated room, making sure that all pets and food are right out of the way. Do not breath in the vapours from these cans, as they are very often *highly toxic*. Do not smoke while spraying and do not work near naked flames.

ANTS

Ants are mostly likely to bother you during the summer. They are attracted into the house by sweet, sticky things, fat and grease. Black ants are the most common type to come into the home. Watch them to find out where there nest is located and then destroy it with a kettle of boiling water poured down the entrance hole. If they  continue coming in, try to find their point of entry and stuff it with cotton wool soaked in paraffin. There are many proprietary products on the market for getting rid of ants. Some will be taken back into the nests and thus kill a whole colony, others are more localized.

If you are really desperate about getting them out of the house but cannot obtain any insecticide, use small sponges soaked in sweet water to attract them and to keep them busy. When there are a number collected together on the sponge pick it up and pour boiling water over it. This will kill them outright.

Protect food from attack by putting it on a table and then standing the table legs in bowls of water. The ants will not be able to cross the water.

If you are sure that the children and pets will not get hold of it, make a solution of pouring consistency with 2 cups of borax, 1 cup of sugar and water, then sprinkle outside around the house. This will both attract ants and kill them.

BEDBUGS

Bedbugs are wingless, minute brown insects that live almost anywhere in old houses and furniture. They are active at night and leave a small itchy bite. They may have been resident in the cracks of the floor and in the wallpaper for some time or they may be brought in with mattresses and old furniture.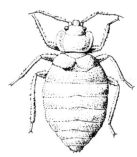
In order to rid the bed of them it is necessary to spray all the parts including the iron work with a suitable insecticide. Spray the mattress as well but be sure not to saturate it. If you have an idea where bedbugs may be lurking, such as the skirting boards, then spray those too. In severe cases, the local health authority will help.

BEES AND WASPS

Bees and wasps usually make their nests in gardens but occasionally they will choose the pipework or under the eaves or similar places around the house. If there is a wasps' or bees' nest near the house, then it is in your interests to destroy it without delay. Contact your local health authority for advice. If a
swarm has settled in your house, then it will need a professional to shift it. Call the local health authority for help. Do not disturb the nest under any circumstances.

BOOK LICE

These are off-white insects that feed on mould and damp in books, paper, cardboard and plaster. They do not like dry, warm conditions so expose the area to the highest temperature possible or spray with a preparation for crawling insects. Do not keep up the heat, however, as it is bad for book bindings.

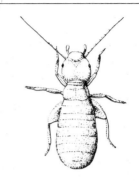

CARPET BEETLES

It is the grubs of this insect, rather than the insect itself, that are the pest. They will feed on carpets, feathers and wool. They may come from birds' nests in the attic and will travel to a warm area wherever there is food. You will find that they leave small holes in the fabric. Treat with a proprietary insecticide.

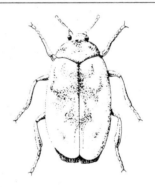

COCKROACHES

These come out at night and eat food, starch, fabric and paper. They are carriers of food poisoning and will infect any food or surface that they have walked across. They can be very difficult to get rid of. Spray the roaches themselves with an insecticide and then their haunts and any

routes that they use. If you find the problem is getting worse and you are unable to get rid of them then contact the health authorities who will come in and fumigate the house.

To prevent cockroaches reappearing, sprinkle boric acid powder along the areas where they appeared before. The acid acts slowly but does eventually kill the roaches. Use it with caution (see Silverfish entry).

EARWIGS

These look unpleasant, but do no damage. They do not live naturally in the house but sometimes are found in quite large numbers. They have probably been brought in from the garden. If necessary squirt with an insecticidal powder and then brush them up.

FLEAS

These are a common pest in homes where there are either cats or dogs. Cat fleas will actually infest human beings. Dog fleas tend to stick to dogs. Dog fleas carry the eggs of the tapeworm, so if the dog eats the fleas it will become infected. The fleas' bites cause areas of irritation, formed around a red spot.

They are spaced wider apart than mosquito bites and are often in a long series. Check your pet for fleas. You should be able to see them running about in the fur. It may also be infested with the eggs, which look like dandruff. It is at this point that you should spray the pet with a proprietary product. Follow the manufacturer's instructions, avoiding the pet's eyes. Give it a flea collar once it has been treated as this will make sure that it will not get re-infested. Treat bedding and furniture as well.

It is not a good idea to de-infest young kittens. Wait until they are at least three months old.

Vacuum thoroughly after you have treated the carpets and furniture for fleas as the eggs may well lay dormant for two months. Destroy the cleaner bag after use.

FLIES

Flies really are the most unpleasant of the household pests. They trail about in rotting meat, and in dung and then, if allowed to settle, will regurgitate on to food or any surface. They carry over thirty different diseases, and lay their eggs at an alarming rate during the summer. Prevention is the best remedy to
the fly problem. Keep general hygiene high in the kitchen.

Do not leave food around to rot. Crumbs are also an attraction, as is pet food.

Keep the lid firmly on both your outdoor dustbin and your indoor one.

If flies are swarming around your dustbin, wash it down with some warm water, allow to dry and then sprinkle soap powder in the dustbin.

Mothballs placed on the outside and inside of your dustbin will discourage flies and other insects from showing an interest in its contents.

Keep any garden manure well away from the house as flies are attracted to it and will swarm around it.

Use insecticides carefully as some strips should not be placed in a room used by elderly people or young children. Read the instructions.

Rub the flies' settling points with oil of lavender as they find this smell repellant.

Many herbs from the garden will act as insect repellants around the house. They can be made up as an alternative to lavender bags. Try using cloves, chamomile, basil, mint, tandy, for example.

Bay leaves in the larder will discourage flies and last for a year or more. Leave them on the branch and then use them for cooking when you need them.

MICE

Mice can be dangerous pests as they carry salmonella and if allowed to reach your food can infect it. They can be heard scratching around in the woodwork, or you may see their small, brown droppings around the house. They have very sharp teeth which they need to keep that way, so they will chew through  most things including electricity cables, packets and newspapers. They breed at a great rate and it is not long before a minor problem becomes a major infestation, so get rid of them as quickly as possible. Your local health authority will be able to help. Sometimes the smell of a cat will get rid of them. Try borrowing a friend's pet. If this fails, then either trap them or put down rodenticide. Try using a trap first as rodenticide is *poisonous*.

If you do use a rodenticide follow the manufacturer's instructions *to the letter*, and try, if possible, to isolate the area that is being treated by locking up the room, so that pets and children are really safe.

Put anything other than cheese in a mouse trap as they do not particularly like it. They are much more fond of chocolate, nuts and peanut butter.

Mice do not like the smell of fresh mint. If you have sprigs of peppermint in the garden, scatter them around the areas affected by the mice; or use oil of peppermint. Saturate paper with it, and place in mouse-affected areas.

110

MITES

There are a variety of mites in the house, mostly so small they are seldom seen, unless they catch your eye when they move. The house or furniture mite may be found in old upholstery, especially if it is damp. Treat as for book lice. Dust mites are ubiquitous. Though harmless, some people are allergic to them.

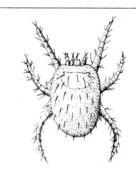

MOSQUITOES

These breed in stagnant water. If you can get them while they are still breeding, drop a spot of paraffin into the water to kill the larvae. If mosquitoes are annoying you outdoors, light a cigarette or a couple of candles as they do not like smoke. Nor do they like basil so keep a pot of it in places they frequent.

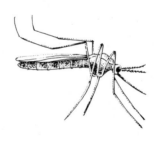

MOTHS

It is the moth larvae that actually do the damage to cloth. They are most often found in the folds of the cloth and are surrounded by a fluffy substance. The first thing to do is to brush the larvae off the material. They attack natural fibres, especially wool, and are cap-

able of eating the wool out of a wool and synthetic mix.

If you find the larvae eating the carpet, the best way to destroy them is to steam them to death with a warm iron and a damp cloth. Once you have removed the larvae treat the carpet with an aerosol preparation that will protect the carpet from further damage.

Never put anything away with greasy stains on it, as moths will be attracted to the grease.

If you find that clothing is being attacked by moths, remove the larvae, bearing in mind that they may be tucked under pocket and collar flaps. Then clear the drawer, checking everything else for damage. Use moth-balls to prevent any larvae you may have missed from surviving. Line drawers with newspaper so that the larvae cannot get back in through the bottom of the drawer.

Epsom salts sprinkled among garments in long storage will help make sure that the clothes are not attacked by moths.

If you are winding knitting wool for long-term storage then wind it around a central ball of camphor.

PLASTER BEETLES

Found in damp plaster in either new or old houses: they are a dark colour and about 2 mm ($\frac{1}{10}$ inch) long. They feed off the mould that grows on the damp plaster and should disappear when the mould dries out. They may be a sign of a damp spot you didn't know about.

RATS

Rats represent a grave health risk as they carry many diseases. They are encouraged to appear where there is food or rubbish left lying around which they will use to make nests with. There are two types of common rat – the sewer rat and the water rat. They are larger than mice, have longer tails and can grow to 23 cm (9 inches) or more. There are many poisonous rat baits available but they must be used with great care.

If you are unable to deal with the problem yourself then get in touch with the health authorities. They will come and get rid of them. If you do succeed in killing a rat, make sure that you either bury it deep in the garden or burn it.

SILVERFISH

They appear in damp areas of the house; usually around the bathroom. If they come from other areas this may indicate a problem with damp that you do not know about. They are small, wingless insects with cigar-shaped bodies that move quickly. They feed off starch and glue that they find around the

house and can be harmful to books. Use an insecticide, or sprinkle boric acid mixed with a little sugar, around the places they come from. However, do not use boric acid if there is a possibility that children or dogs will touch it.

SPIDERS

These are much maligned as they do no harm and in fact will rid your house or crawling insects as well as flies. If you do not like touching them but still wish to remove them, open the window or door in readiness, and use a long-handled mop or broom. Once the spider has crawled on to the end, take it to the outside and shake. Alternatively, you can use a piece of paper in the same way, if you don't mind coming close to a spider. Or, place a glass over the spider once it has crawled inside, cover the bottom of the glass with a piece of paper, then take it outside, uncover it and leave the spider to crawl out.

WEEVILS

These are small beetles with long noses. Some eat food, others live on wood (see Woodworm). Those which are food-eating may be found in flour or bread although they are not very common. Any products affected should be returned to the shop. Then spray all round with an insecticide.

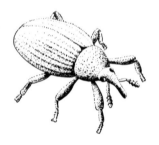

WOODWORM

These are the grub of the furniture beetle and will appear accompanied by holes and piles of fresh sawdust. They attack any kind of wood, new or old, so check wood floors and furniture when you are cleaning. Small areas can be treated with a proprietary fluid from hardware or DIY

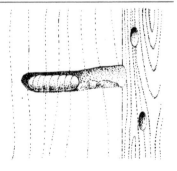

stores. Follow the instructions that come with the fluid. Do not inhale the fumes and do not let it splash on the skin. If possible work in the open air and wear overalls to protect your clothing.

If you find that the infestation is in structural beams of the house or that it covers a large area, then it is essential that you call in professional help. Use someone well known, who will be around to keep to a guarantee, which will usually last about twenty years.

As a precaution, check any second-hand or antique furniture that you bring into the house for signs of fresh woodworm activity.

"Cut Your Coat According To Your Cloth"

Hints on fabrics and fabric care

Cleaning labels
and codes

CARE LABELS

It's the law: Manufacturers must, by law, label all garments and state the type of material they are made from. Many manufacturers also add the care labels which correspond to internationally agreed washing and care symbols. This should mean that it is possible to understand the care of foreign-made clothes as well as British clothes. It is as well to understand these labels as they provide information about fabric care and how to keep the material in its best condition. This is important, as many fabrics must be washed at the recommended temperature to get them really clean.

This symbol gives the recommended washing instructions.

This symbol means do not machine wash.

The figure above the line indicates the machine code that the fabric should be washed at. This may correspond with your washing machine. These are also shown on the side of the detergent pack. The temperature shown below the line is a guide for water temperature.

This indicates that the article must not be washed.

This indicates that the article can be bleached with chlorine bleach in solution.

Do not use bleach on garments bearing this sign.

The circle indicates that the garment should be dry-cleaned only.

The letter inside the circle indicates the kind of dry cleaning fluid that should be used on the garment (see below). This will not concern you unless you are attempting to clean it in a laundrette dry cleaning machine, in which case you should check that the symbols correspond with fluid in the machine you are using (see page 120).

This symbol provides you with a guide to ironing the garment.

One dot means use a cool iron on such fabrics as acrylic, nylon, acetate, polyester and viscose.

Two dots mean use a warm iron. This should be used on such fabric as polyester mixes and wool fibres.

Three dots indicate a very hot setting which should only be used on cotton and linen.

This indicates that the article should not be ironed because it would harm it to do so.

This symbol indicates the drying instructions.

Tumble dry.   Line dry.

Drip dry.   Dry flat.

If the dry cleaning symbol has an A in its circle then any type of dry cleaning fluid can be used. This is useful if you want to use the laundrette dry cleaning machine.

in the circle means that many dry cleaning solvents can be used, i.e. you can use a laundrette machine. Both these symbols mean that any dry cleaner can cope with the garment.

in the circle and a line underneath means do not use a laundrette machine and that cleaners should be made aware of the symbol as certain precautions have to be taken.

indicates that only a certain number of cleaners will be able to deal with this. It usually appears on a delicate fabric. When you take a garment into a cleaners bearing this sign, point it out to the cleaner and ask if he has the chemical. It indicates that solvent 113 should be used on the garment.

Aftercare: After either dry cleaning the clothes yourself, or having them cleaned, make sure that they are well aired before they are put away as the fumes are quite poisonous. Articles you should never dry clean yourself include padded materials, duvets, or anything that is likely to house the fumes for a long time.

FABRIC CARE

Wash programmes: There are nine basic wash programmes. Most modern automatic washing machines are designed and labelled to cope with them. You will also find these symbols on most packets of washing powder. The temperature in the tub symbol indicates the water heat for machines. Corresponding details for washing by hand are also given. Codes 8 and 9 are later additions, usually only seen on foreign clothes. The codes are part of the International Textile Care Labelling Code.

Wash code	1 95°	2 60°	3 60°	4 50°	5 40°	6 40°	7 40°	8 30°	9 95°
Machine Washing	Very hot to boil Maximum wash	Hot Maximum wash	Hot Medium wash	Hand-hot Medium wash	Warm Medium wash	Warm Minimum wash	Warm Minimum wash	Cool Minimum wash	Very hot (95°C) to boil
Hand Washing	Hand-hot (50°C) or boil	Hand-hot (50°C)	Hand-hot (50°C)	Hand-hot	Warm	Warm	Warm Do not rub	Cool	Hand-hot (50°C) or boil
Agitation	Maximum	Maximum	Medium	Medium	Maximum	Minimum	Minimum Do not rub	Minimum	Medium
Rinsing, spinning, wringing	Spin or wring	Spin or wring	Cold rinse Short spin or drip-dry	Cold rinse Short spin or drip-dry	Spin or wring	Cold rinse Short spin Do not wring	Spin Do not hand wring	Cold rinse Short spin Do not wring	Cold rinse Drip-dry
Suitable fabrics	White cotton and linen fabrics without special finishes	Cotton, linen or viscose fabrics without special finishes and colour-fast at 60°C	White nylon; white polyester/ cotton fabrics	Coloured nylon, polyester special finish cotton and viscose; acrylic cotton; coloured polyester cotton	Machine washable wool, cotton, linen or viscose fabrics with colours fast at 40°C but not at 60°C	Acrylics; acetate and triacetate, including mixtures with wool; polyester/ wool blends	Wool, including blankets and wool mixtures with cotton or viscose; silk	Silk and printed acetate fabrics with colours not fast at 40°C	Cotton articles with special finishes capable of being boiled, but requiring drip-drying

A-Z of fabrics and fabric care

ACETATE

Normally used for lining other fabric. Looks silky, but can come in other textures. Washing instructions depend on what fabric the acetate is lining. Acetate itself can be washed on wash code 6 or 8. Wool lined with acetate mixtures should be hand washed carefully. Use warm water with a cold rinse and a short spin. It myst not be wrung.

Iron while still damp but re-soak the whole garment if it gets too dry. Do not sprinkle water on it or the finish will be blotchy.

Acetate is dissolved by solvent stain removers, and by vinegar, so never use them in an attempt to remove stains.

ACRYLIC

Usually used to simulate fine wool. It is a synthetic material; soft and durable and easier to wash than wool. Follow the care label on the garment – it can usually be machine washed on code 6. Beware, however, of using too high washing temperatures, anything above 40°C/104°F will set in creases that never come out.

It is sensible to wash acrylic garments often, and well, before the dirt becomes impregnated. To wash by hand (some acrylic/wool mixes need treating this way) use warm water, but be careful in handling while wet. Do not twist or agitate too much.

A cold rinse will help to stop any creasing in acrylics, but be sure either to do a very short spin, or to treat as wool and lay between towels and then roll, or you will put fresh creases in.

Do not hang up to drip-dry, or the garment will be lengthened by its own weight. Dry as for wool, flat.

Never iron acrylic when it is slightly damp, otherwise it will stretch out of shape. Wait patiently until it is completely dry. If the fabric is pleated, then rinse in warm water and drip-dry. Do not bleach.

ANGORA

Rabbit fur wool, has a very fluffy appearance. It is often mixed with other materials to give it strength and to make it easier to care for. Wash as for wool.

BATISTE

A very lightweight fabric used to make underwear, linings and shirts. It is made from a variety of fabrics usually cotton, silk or viscose and must be washed according to the material from which it is made.

BOUCLÉ

This has a bobbly surface made up of loops of fibres, and is often used in knitted garments. It can also come in fabric form, and in a variety of materials, such as wool, cotton and synthetic fibres. It should, therefore, be washed according to its care label for the fabric used. If you are unsure of its treatment, dry clean.

BRAID

Braid trimmings should not be washed. If you want to wash the garment they are on, then first remove the trimmings. Silver braid can be cleaned with dry bicarbonate of soda. Make sure that the powder gets well into all the crevices. It will take some time to absorb the dirt so leave on for as long as possible. Take off again with a stiff brush, or an old toothbrush. To clean gold braid, use a mix of dry cream of tartar and stale breadcrumbs. Leave on as before, then remove with a stiff brush.

BROCADE

The raised surface on this decorative border material makes it difficult to wash successfully. It is woven from several different fibres, some silky, so it must be dry-cleaned.

BRODERIE ANGLAISE

Most broderie anglaise is used as a border on cotton material. Unless it is very delicate it can be washed with other cotton garments. Check first that the material it is attached to is cotton. If it is very delicate, wash by hand.

BUMP

This cotton curtain lining material cannot be washed as it is not of very high quality. Dry clean.

CALICO

Calico is usually made from pure cotton, but, on occasions, can be mixed with synthetic material. It is uncoloured and has a slightly rough texture to it. Wash as for cotton when it is a synthetic mix. If you need to whiten calico, do so in the first wash by adding a drop of white spirit to the water.

CAMBRIC

Cotton fabric with a smooth appearance. Wash as for cotton and starch to restore its slightly stiff appearance.

CANDLEWICK

This is used for making bedspreads and dressing gowns because of its warmth. It comes in a variety of colours and the tufts make a variety of patterns. Used to be made entirely from cotton, but now, to reduce the price, it is often mixed with synthetic fibres. Wash according to the more delicate fibre. Shake well after washing to restore the pile.

CANVAS

Canvas is a very strong fabric mainly used for making bags and for upholstery. It has a slightly rough finish and is usually left in its natural colour. Wash with detergent and warm water. Scrub with a nail brush to remove stubborn marks. Now made from a variety of fibres including cotton and synthetic.

CHALLIS

An expensive but beautiful fabric made from wool. Wash as for wool but by hand only.

CHEESECLOTH

A fabric that was not much used for clothing until it became fashionable a few years ago. Very lightweight and loosely woven. Made from cotton, or cotton mixture, it must be hand washed to keep its shape. Do not wring but use towels to absorb the moisture. Iron while damp, stretching into shape as you do so.

CHENILLE

This is used for heavy curtains and tablecloths; can be pure silk or synthetic. Clean according to the fibres used to make the chenille. It has a raised pile and often comes in very plush colours, which may run in the wash so wash separately at first. If the chenille is very old, the material is often rather delicate, so it is preferable to wash carefully by hand or dry clean.

CHIFFON

A very soft, sheer fabric made from silk or synthetic fibres. If it is made from viscose or silk, it is best to have it dry-cleaned; otherwise wash according to the fibre type. Iron while still damp. This will give you an opportunity to ease the fabric back into its original shape.

CHINTZ

This is cotton with a glazed finish on its right side. It is traditionally printed with flowers and used for furnishings. Old chintz should be dry-cleaned. Modern fabric can be washed, but should be treated carefully when still wet. Do not rub or twist. Do not treat with starch. The final rinse must be cold to prevent excessive creasing. Iron while still damp.

CIRE

Ciré is a synthetic material, often made from nylon, and has a shiny finish. It should be hand washed.

CORDUROY

A very hard wearing fabric with a soft, velvety raised pile. It is used for upholstery and for garments. Made from a cotton or a cotton mix. Best washed by hand according to the mixture. Rough treatment when wet will harm the pile. Do not wring or twist. While the material is drying, smooth the pile in the right direction with a soft clean cloth. Shake well. Iron on the wrong side while still slightly damp using a warm iron.

COTTON

A versatile fabric, strong and easy to care for. Comes in such a variety of weaves and finishes that it is essential to follow any instructions that come with the material. Used for almost anything – upholstery, clothing, fabrics, curtains – it also comes in a variety of mixes with synthetic fibres. Can have special finishes to make it waterproof or flameproof.

White cotton can be boiled to keep it white.

Cotton shirts and blouses may have a 'dressing' in the fabric which will form a scum when the detergent gets to it. You can remove a lot of the dressing by soaking the garment in cold water for 30 minutes before putting it in the washing machine.

Most colourfast cottons will stand a hot water wash. However, even colourfast cottons sometimes bleed slightly at every wash so it is safest to wash them separately. Detergent, not soap, should be used on flame-resistant finishes.

CRÊPE AND CRÊPE DE CHINE

Crêpe is usually thin with a wrinkled, bumpy texture and is made from a variety of fabrics. Some crêpes have to be dry cleaned, so follow the care label. Otherwise wash in warm water by hand. Crêpe must be ironed on the wrong side while still damp. Crêpe de Chine is of lighter weight with a slight shine. Made from silk or synthetic fibres. Treat according to the fabric, iron on the wrong side when damp.

DAMASK

A fancy fabric with a design woven into the fabric in shiny thread. Made from a variety of fibres including silk, and synthetic materials. Treat according to fabric.

DENIM

Usually made from cotton, although it does now appear in synthetic mixes, with white warp thread and coloured, usually blue, weft thread. Hard-wearing but it does shrink in the wash. Tends to wear in patches and the colour fades. Wash on its own as the colour never really becomes fast. Iron while still damp.

DRILL

This has a slightly raised surface, but is useful for clothes that get a lot of use, as it wears well. Wash as for cotton.

FELT

Made from matted fibres of thick wool. Felt cannot be washed as it shrinks very easily. Dry clean only.

FLANNEL

This is usually a woollen fabric with a choice of finishes that are either smooth or slightly raised. Anything large or precious should be taken to the dry cleaners; otherwise wash very gently as for wool.

GABARDINE

This fabric is used mostly for raincoats and outdoor coats. It is a woven fabric, often made of a blend of fibres. Often treated with a water-resistant finish. Should only be dry-cleaned.

GINGHAM

Old-fashioned checked cotton fabric, but can now be made from a fibre mix. Wash accordingly. Iron back into shape when still damp.

HESSIAN

A rough fabric made with an open weave. Hard-wearing and made from natural fibres, it has a variety of uses. It can even be used as a wall covering. This material must be dry-cleaned.

JERSEY

This fabric has a knitted surface and stretches. It is made from a number of different fibres, including expensive wool, which must be dry-cleaned. Viscose jersey should also be dry-cleaned. Synthetic types should be washed according to the label. Do not twist. A short spin will not do it any harm. Dry as wool.

LACE

Lace can be made from a variety of materials, some are synthetic. If it is not delicate, then wash as for the fibre it is made from. Old lace is difficult to wash without the risk of damaging it so if the article is valuable, consult a specialist cleaner. However, delicate lace can be soaked in plain distilled water for several hours to lift the grime.

Less fine or valuable lace can be washed in pure soap suds but avoid stretching and squeezing the lace as this can ruin its shape. Rinse well, then lay the lace out and blot with a towel.

Lace curtains can be folded and put inside a cotton pillow case for washing in pure soap suds.

LAWN

A very fine soft cotton or cotton and synthetic mix. Wash by hand and spin gently. Can be ironed while still damp on the wrong side.

LEATHER

Coats and jackets: Stains should not be treated at home because solvents can often take the colour out of leather and leave a lighter patch. Take the garment to a dry cleaner who specializes in cleaning leather and explain what has caused the stain, so that they know how to deal with it. Always make sure buttons are securely fixed because if they match the coat, as is often the case, a replacement can be impossible to get.

Any tiny tears in the leather can be repaired by carefully sticking the material which has lifted off back down with a touch of clear glue. A match is ideal for pushing the surface piece firmly back down on to the skin.

Always have garments cleaned regularly and before they become too soiled.

Different kinds of leather: The different kinds of leathers used in bags and shoes need quite individual care and attention. White buckskin needs a good brush to get rid of any surplus dust, then should be cleaned with any of the proprietary brands sold for the purpose. Do not dry calf near heat as it may become dry and stiff. Buff crocodile shoes with a soft cloth after wearing and you will only need to use shoe cream occasionally. Lizard is designed for the lazy, since you just remove any dust or dirt with a soft brush and give a quick wipe with a soft dry duster. Pigskin needs fairly rough treatment. Use a wire brush after wearing and a suede cleaner from time to time.

LINEN

An expensive fabric, as it is made from natural fibre flax, linen is very strong and hard-wearing and is used for table cloths and napkins as well as garments. It is possible to wash colourfast linen on codes 1 or 2 but check the care label. If you want to hand wash, use hot soapy water and treat as cotton. Linen can be boiled to restore its whiteness, but it may shrink. Iron with a hot iron on the wrong side when still damp, as this is the only way to get the creases out. Once the fabric is dry, creases are impossible to remove.

MOHAIR

This fibre comes from the angora goat. It has to be washed as for wool, although some mixtures may take other treatment. Check care label for details. Do not wash mohair jumpers too often as it is difficult to prevent them from furring badly.

MOIRÉ

Moiré is usually made from silk, although demand has meant the introduction of other fibres. The fabric is water-marked in great swirls with a raised surface. It can only be dry-cleaned.

MUSLIN

Originally used in the dairy for straining cheese, it is now used as a fashion material. It has a large open weave and is usually slightly sheer. It should be hand-washed as cheese-cloth. Iron while still damp.

NET

An open mesh fabric with many uses, though principally as curtaining. Comes now in a variety of fibres, usually synthetic. Net curtains should be shaken well before washing as the dirt tends to get stuck in the holes. Wash them in plenty of warm soapy water, so that they can be gently moved around. The bath is often the best place as a small bowl may cause the nets to become creased. Curtains that have become dingy may well respond to a nylon whitener sold specially for nets.

One old-fashioned remedy for making fine nets look crisper is to dip the freshly-washed nets in a solution of 1 tablespoon of sugar and ½litre (1 pint) of water. Hang the nets at the window while still slightly damp to allow the creases to drop and so avoid ironing.

NYLON

A synthetic fibre which is strong, tough and versatile. Used in clothes. Follow the care label. Most nylon can be machine washed at code 3 for whites, and 4 for coloureds. Wash by hand in hand hot water. Make sure that the water is not too hot otherwise white nylon starts to take on a greyish tinge. Never use bleach on nylon. Use a cold rinse to ensure that you get a crease-free finish. If treated properly nylon should not need to be ironed. If it is necessary, then iron with a warm iron while still slightly damp.

OILSKIN

Used for rainwear and for tablecloths, it is treated with oil and has a shiny surface. Clean by wiping with a damp cloth.

PIQUÉ

A strong cotton or synthetic material with a raised design. Wash according to fibre, shake to raise the pile, and then iron on the back on a thick clean cloth to protect the pile from flattening.

POLYESTER

A synthetic fibre, though sometimes blended with natural fibres, it is easy to care for and very versatile, lending itself to woven or knitted textures. Machine wash according to the label. Most polyesters will machine wash at code 3 for white and 4 for coloureds. Hand washing should be done in hand hot water. Water above that temperature will damage the fibres. Never boil. A cold rinse and a short spin will ensure that there are few creases. Some fabrics, especially those with pleats, are best drip-dried – study the care label. A cool iron will get rid of any creases when the fabric is dry.

POPLIN

Usually a cotton fabric, woven with a fairly smooth finish, now produced in synthetic fibres too. Must be washed according to the fibre type. See under fabric heading.

SAILCLOTH

A very strong cotton or cotton mix fabric. Wash according to the fibre.

SATIN

A luxurious, smooth, shiny fabric, originally made from closely woven silk fibres, but now more often, and more cheaply, made from synthetic fibres. Dress satin can usually be washed according to the fibre it is made of. The heavier upholstery satin must be dry cleaned. Iron with a cool iron on the wrong side while still damp to restore the shiny finish.

SEERSUCKER

A cotton or cotton mix with a bumpy crinkly finish to it, it comes in very bright colours and stripes. Wash according to the fibre content. There is no need to iron.

SERGE

A very strong hard-wearing fabric, principally used for clothes, such as uniforms, that need to last a long time. Originally serge was made from pure wool, but now it is mixed with cotton or synthetic fibres which give it a longer life. Study the care label. It should be dry-cleaned.

SHANTUNG

Originally the name for wild silk material with bobbly threads, giving a very uneven surface. Now imitated with synthetic fibres. Wash according to the fibre content. Iron on the wrong side when completely dry.

SILK

A delicate natural fibre with a beautiful feel and appearance. Must be hand washed to prevent damage. Do not boil or soak. Wash in hand-hot water, squeezing the soap through the material as you do for wool. The temperature of the rinsing water should be the same as for washing. Put the silk between two towels to absorb the moisture. Do not wring. Iron while still slightly damp on the wrong side.

Do not allow silk to become heavily soiled; perspiration stains are almost impossible to remove. Do not rub silk while wet, as this is when it is in its weakest state. Anything that is badly stained should be dry-cleaned before the stain is set.

SUEDE

Always follow the manufacturer's instructions. You can never hope to clean suede jackets and coats successfully at home, so don't try. However, you can cope with the odd mark. Fuller's earth well rubbed into the surface, then left in for ten minutes before brushing out with a soft brush (NEVER a wire suede brush) may do the trick. If the skin is tired looking, hold the area over a bowl of boiling water, let the steam penetrate and brush up the nap with a rubber brush.

TAFFETA

This is traditionally made from silk but now more often produced in synthetic fabrics. If the taffeta is made from silk then send it to be dry-cleaned, or treat according to the label. Most man-made taffeta can be washed but must be handled gently. Use a mild detergent and warm water, squeezing the soap through the material. Use a cold water rinse and hang up to drip-dry. Iron while still damp on the wrong side.

TOWELLING

This is usually 100% cotton with a looped weave designed to have high absorbency. It can be machine or hand-washed according to the care label. If you are washing towels in the machine, reduce your normal washload, since towels need more room to ensure adequate rinsing. Deep colours have to be washed separately, as a rule, at least for the first few washes. They can be spun or wrung dry. Terry towelling used for nappies should be washed at a very high temperature and thoroughly rinsed. Fabric conditioner will keep them soft.

TWEED

This material is traditionally made with wool, usually used for suits, coats or skirts. If it is woollen then it must be treated according to the care label or dry-cleaned. If it is made from synthetic fibres it should be possible to wash carefully according to the fibre content. Check with the care label.

VELOUR

A velvety fabric, now widely used for dresses, it is lighter and more flexible than velvet, but with the same rich appearance. It is made in a variety of materials both natural and synthetic. Treat according to the care label. If it is crushed, treat as for velvet.

VELVET

An expensive, but luxurious, fabric which is now available in many fibres, some of which are easy to care for. Cotton velvet and silk velvet should be dry-cleaned, especially if you are unsure of its fibre content. If the care label indicates that it is washable, follow the instructions and drip-dry. If it is necessary to iron velvet, then do so over a number of thick towels to avoid crushing the pile; or, even better, hang the garment in the bathroom while someone is running a bath. This should straighten out any creases. If the pile becomes crushed, then hold the fabric over a steaming saucepan or kettle for a few minutes. This should perk it up again.

VISCOSE

This is used extensively to imitate natural fibres cheaply. It must be handled with care. Treat as for wool, squeezing the detergent through the material. Avoid wringing or rough handling. Iron while still damp on the wrong side. Do not press along the seams or marks will be left on the surface.

VIYELLA

This is a brand name for a soft cotton and wool mix and must be washed very gently by hand and treated as wool. Iron while still damp on the wrong side.

VOILE

A floaty, sheer fabric which can be made from synthetic or natural fibres. Treat according to the care label or according to the fabric. Do not wring, but roll up in a towel to get rid of the moisture. Iron very gently while still damp.

WOOL

This requires great care in its handling and in its washing in order to preserve its special qualities. It is the warmest and the softest of all the fabrics available, and is widely used in the manufacture of every type of garment. It is very versatile and can be knitted or woven and it is also used in conjunction with other fibres.

Always wash wools according to the instructions on the label. Unless it says 'machine washable' they should be given a gentle handwash, with as little rubbing as possible. Turn the garment inside out as this will mean less damage to the surface of the wool. To keep the shape, fasten all the buttons.

Any very special sweaters which you don't want to run the risk of spoiling can be washed with a special cold water solution. You can buy it in powder form in small packets. A small amount of glycerine ($1\frac{1}{2}$ teaspoons) in the rinsing water gives wool a nice soft texture and keeps it bouncy.

Wool clothes do not need to be dried flat; they are surprisingly robust garments and can be hung on the line. Take a pair of old tights and put them in one sleeve, right through the garment and out the end of the other sleeve and peg the tights, not the wool, to the line. Incidentally, do fasten buttons and zips before you hang wool garments up.

However, particularly heavy items may not be suitable for hanging up in case the weight of the garment stretches them. To be absolutely sure that a sweater is the same size and shape *after* drying, you can draw its outline on a piece of wrapping paper before you wash it, then when it's ready to dry, put it down over the pencilled outline and gently pull it into the required shape as necessary.

Any seams which have become slightly rucked, or button-hole bands on cardigans which have wrinkled in the wash, can also be pulled back to their proper length just before the drying stage.

Garments made from wool will lose their bounce if you iron them and it shouldn't be necessary anyway, but you can re-fashion a woolly which has become somewhat shapeless by using a steam iron. This is an 'at-a-distance' ironing technique where the metal never actually touches the material.

You may need a surface slightly larger than your ironing board for this. The kitchen table, well covered by a thick blanket, may be suitable. Stretch the garment to the desired shape and fasten it down with pins. Hold your iron half an inch above the wool and let the steam penetrate. Move slowly over the whole surface.

Sometimes the cause can also prove to be the cure! For instance, shine on the seats of skirts and trousers is often caused by ironing. The 'at-a-distance' ironing technique can often remove the shine. Hold the iron about an inch above the material, let the steam penetrate for a few minutes and brush lightly with a very soft brush.

Wool cellular blankets may be better dry-cleaned than washed ordinarily. If this is the case, it will be shown on the care label.

WINCEYETTE

This is a brand name for a soft fabric with a slightly woolly finish, made most commonly in cotton, wool and viscose. It should be treated as wool.

"It's No Use Crying Over Spilt Milk"

How to deal
with all types of stains

Stain removal: 11 general principles

1. Tackle any stain immediately, because once a substance has had a chance to get right into the fabric it can stubbornly remain there. If you're at home, there's no excuse at all for not doing a thorough job – drop everything to see to the stain. If the waiter spills wine on your skirt, don't just mutter that it doesn't matter and dab at it ineffectually with your hanky, insist on the mark being removed there and then (a spoonful of salt from the kitchen, for instance, will stop wine spreading further over fabric).

2. It's useful to memorize the three broad categories of stains and the general treatment of each. Basically, there are greasy stains, water-soluble stains and protein stains. The first usually take to treatment with grease solvents of one sort or another and to hot soapy water; the second respond to the cold water sponge and a slick of soap if needed; the third can be dealt with by cold water and biological powders. But that's only a rough guide to help you cope in an emergency. Many fabrics can't be washed and so all sorts of other substances like borax or vinegar have to be brought into use. The stain removal chart goes into all this in detail, see pages 147 to 176.

3. Try to keep a few bits and pieces together to make up a stain removing kit which will be readily to hand when you need it. Small sponges, for instance, are ideal for applying remedial treatment to some stains, so buy one large one and cut it up into several pieces. Keep the sponges in a box along with a pad of some material to put behind stains (this saves you resorting to a towel and ending up with a stain on that, too), a few paper tissues for blotting up moisture, a couple of men's old hankies, a small clothes brush and a wad of cotton wool which is useful as a 'pad' if you don't have a proper one, to mop up excess moisture and it can also come in handy for applying soap and water or solvents. A medicine dropper or small syringe is useful to avoid overwetting with detergent or solvents. It can also be used to squirt liquid through a cloth to remove a stain on to a backing pad. Put these various items, and any extras you can think of yourself, in a polythene bag or an old plastic ice cream carton and keep it under the kitchen sink, in the bathroom or some other such readily accessible place.

4. There's a right and a wrong way to use solvents and this is the right way: deal with the stain from the *wrong* side of the garment and use a pad on the other side to absorb the substance. That way you are pushing the substance from the surface of the fabric straight on to the pad and if there are any stubborn little traces left they will be on the wrong side and not visible. Dampen a pad of cloth with some of the solvent. Make a ring with the moistened pad a few centimetres outside the actual stain where the fabric is clean, then work inwards. Do it the other way round and you run the risk of a 'ring' being left round the outside of the stain which will mean the whole garment having to be washed or dry cleaned.

5. Even in the middle of winter work fairly near to an open window when you are treating stains with some of the solvents and chemicals needed for the job – that way you'll avoid getting the full blast of the fumes which will escape out of the window instead.

6. Acetates, viscose, delicate materials and coloureds can be totally unpredictable in their reaction to cleaning chemicals, so always test any chemical you plan to use on a hidden part of the garment which won't be seen if you do damage to the fabric or the colour. The overlap left at seams is a good test spot; avoid hems whenever possible, because you never know when you might want to let them down!

7. Don't ever soak garments made of wool, silk or with a flame-proof finish in an attempt to get a stain out; you may get the stain out but you'll ruin the garment.

8. Unless you are sure of what has been spilled and how best to remove it, be very wary of using hot water on a stain. Heat can easily set stains rather than remove them.

9. If you wouldn't normally wash any particular material and you're not sure whether you can or not, then always play safe and try something simple, like plain cold water.

10. Get rid of any stains on clothes before putting them into the laundry basket. Some stains, of course, come out in the wash, but others can become a permanent fixture in the washing process. It's best not to take any chances.

11. Don't try to remove the very last traces of a stubborn stain if you've tried more than twice to remove it. It's better to leave a faint trace of a stain than run the risk of damaging the .fabric by too much rubbing or chemical action.

STAIN REMOVERS FOR YOUR STORE-CUPBOARD

Ammonia is a useful stain removing aid and should generally be used in a diluted form – 1 part ammonia to 3 parts water is the most usual one, though some remedies call for just a few drops of ammonia to be added to washing or rinsing water. Fabric is prone to bleeding when it is treated with ammonia, so be sure to do a colourfast test (see page 141) before you start. Ammonia gives off unpleasant fumes and can burn the skin if it comes into contact with it in an undiluted form, so handle it with care.

Amyl acetate is very like nail varnish remover, but it is safer to use on acetate fabrics. It will dissolve some paints and glues and, of course, nail lacquer. It must be used with great care as it is inflammable.

Biological detergents (also known as enzyme detergents) are specially designed to digest protein based stains such as egg, blood, milk (see also page 140). If you are tackling a bad stain of this type, it is useful to soak the item for some time in biological detergent, but follow the instructions on the packet about water temperature. The colder the water is, the longer the soak needed. For bad stains, it is a good idea to soak through the night. Do not soak wool, silk, or anything that has a special finish in this type of detergent as it is very strong. And do not put anything with metal on it (buttons or clasps, for instance) into biological detergents as it may cause the metal to stain the garment.

Bleach is useful for stains on white cotton or linen. It should always be used diluted – neat bleach could damage the fabric irreparably. The ideal dilution for dabbing on to small stains is 5–10 ml (1–2 teaspoons) of bleach to 1 litre (2 pints) of water. If there is a large area to cover, mix 10 ml (2 teaspooons) of bleach to 10 litres (2½ gallons) of cold water. Soak the item in the solution for up to an hour. Always rinse the item well after dabbing or soaking. To prevent the stain from being bleached lighter than the surrounding fabric, immerse the whole garment in the solution. Thorough rinsing is vital, otherwise there is a danger that the traces of bleach will continue to act on the fabric and damage it badly (see also page 77).

Bleach cannot be used on synthetics, delicate fabrics like wool or silk, or anything with a special finish.

Borax (domestic) comes from the chemist in powdered form. It works well at neutralizing acid stains such as those made by wine and fruit, and it can be used on most fabrics. However, it will start to bleach the colour out of some materials after about 15 minutes, so it should be used with some care. The usual dilution is 1 tablespoon to half a litre (1 pint) of warm water. In some forms of stain removal, particularly on white fabrics, it is sprinkled on to the stain, then the material is stretched over a basin and the stain is flushed out with boiling water.

Eucalyptus oil is a highly effective, highly pungent oil that deals effectively with tar stains.

Glycerine softens stains and is useful if the stain is already set before you discover it. Glycerine should be used diluted in equal parts with warm water.

Hydrogen peroxide is a milder form of bleach and can be bought from a chemist. It is suitable for getting stains off the more delicate fabrics, such as wool and silk, but it must not be used on nylon or on fabrics with special finishes. Hydrogen peroxide generally comes in 20 vol. strength and this is usually diluted to a strength of 1 part hydrogen peroxide to 6 parts of water. White garments can be safely soaked overnight in this solution, but coloured fabrics could start to bleach out after about half an hour.

Lemon is useful for first-aid on stains such as iron-mould.

Methylated spirit will very often take the residual colour out of a stain after it has been treated in other ways. Use neat. Do not use on acetate fabrics.

Proprietary grease solvents and dry cleaners come in liquid, dab-on, paste or spray versions. Follow the manufacturer's instructions and avoid inhaling fumes. Proprietary solvents can dissolve some plastics, rubbers, etc., and may be harmful to the skin, so use them with caution. They are very efficient at removing all forms of grease, but be selective as to which solvent you use for which stain.

Salt removes blood and perspiration stains from most materials and is useful for absorbing fruit stains, etc.

Washing soda is useful for removing greasy stains in some circumstances. It is inclined to be caustic, so use it with care.

White spirit is useful for removing some items, paint stains, for instance. It is very inflammable and poisonous.

144

Stains: special cases

BLANKETS

Check the care label to see if the blanket is washable and make sure you can get it into your washing machine – remember it will weigh considerably more when it is wet. It may pay you to take it to the launderette instead, as many of them have heavy duty machines. Otherwise it is possible to wash a blanket in the bath. Soak first in cold water to remove as much dirt as possible, then wash in warm soapy water. Rinse several times to remove the suds, then drain the water off for an hour or so. Fold the blanket in the bath, squeezing while folding to press out as much water as possible. Hang, still folded, on an airer in the garden and only hang on the line once partly dry.

PILLOWS

Pillows whether filled with foam or feather, can be washed, but drying takes such a long time (especially the feathers) that it is best avoided. Always cover with a pillow case and treat spills and stains quickly. Push the filling away from the affected area and hold it back with an elastic band. Then spot treat the case as necessary. If washing is really necessary, use soap suds in the bath and squeeze the pillow lightly. Rinse well and, if possible, spin dry for a short period. If not, drain well on a folded towel, then hang out to dry. Turn the pillow over and round several times while drying to move the filling around. Only use again when completely dry.

Never dry clean pillows in a coin-operated machine, as the fumes from dry cleaning fluids remain in the filling and are dangerous. Some specialist cleaners will treat pillows.

MATTRESSES

Blood and urine are two frequent stains on mattresses. A bloodstained mattress should be tipped on to its side, then sponged carefully with cold salt water, rinsed and then treated with upholstery shampoo. Urine stains should be sponged off with washing-up liquid in cold water, with a little disinfectant added to the rinse.

DUVETS

Stains should be mopped up as quickly as possible. If the filling is feather or down, it is important to isolate the stain; shake the feathers well away from it and tie them up out of the way. Then treat the stained area according to whatever type of stain it is.

Duvets with a synthetic filling can usually be washed, but check, as with blankets, that your machine will take them. Never attempt to clean a feather duvet in a coin-op dry cleaning machine, as there is a danger that you may be overcome by fumes when you take it back home. Take it instead to a specialist dry cleaner. Avoid further stains by using a washable cover on the duvet.

CARPETS

Some carpets are now sold with a special stain-resistant finish. Most stains can simply be mopped up and blotted, but follow the instructions that come with the carpet. On other carpets, stains are best dealt with immediately. Mop up spills with plenty of tissues or kitchen roll or even tea towels. Cover the spill, then stand on the tissues or kitchen roll to soak up all the spill. Use fresh tissues or move them around if necessary. Continue to do this until no more liquid is being absorbed. You may look a little strange standing on piles of tissues but it is the most effective way of blotting up spills. Often if you act fast enough it can prevent a lasting stain occurring (for more information on carpet stains, see A to Z of Stain Removal, page 147). Test any stain removal treatment on a hidden area first.

A-Z
of stain removal

The advice in this section applies to fabrics, furnishings and carpets. Refer to the individual materials for care of other surfaces.

ACIDS

Flush with running *cold* water. Neutralize with a solution of 1 teaspoon of borax to 600 ml (1 pint) of warm water. If you don't have borax, use bicarbonate of soda in the same proportion. Sponge on the solution, then rinse thoroughly with clear water.

ADHESIVE

There are so many different kinds on the market that, for some of the more unusual kinds, the only solution is to ask the manufacturer's advice. However, try these methods on washable fabrics, furnishings and carpets or, if the material is non-washable, take it to your dry cleaner.

Adhesive tape: Remove with methylated spirit or white spirit.

Animal and fish glues: If the fabric is washable, soak in hot water with a tablespoon of vinegar added to it; for non-washables, dab with a similar solution.

Contact and clear adhesives: Dab gently with acetone or a nail varnish remover. Do NOT use on acetate fabrics, such as Tricel.

Epoxy adhesives: Once hard, there is no way you can tackle them. But if you catch them before they harden, use cellulose thinner or methylated spirit on natural fabrics; lighter fuel on synthetics.

Latex adhesives: These can be removed with a cloth soaked in water while still wet, or scraped off if they have dried. If the stain persists, send for the manufacturer's special solvent or try paint brush cleaner on it, but use with caution. Latex glue on the fingers or on a hard surface can be simply rubbed or rolled off.

Modelling cement: Remove with acetone or non-oily nail polish remover. Don't use on acetate material.

PVA glue: Remove with methylated spirit.

Superglue: Apply cold water immediately, either on a pad or by holding the item under a running tap. Act immediately; superglue sticks in seconds.

ALCOHOL

(SEE **Beer, Wine and Spirits**)

ANIMAL STAINS

Speed is the essence here – all messes should be cleaned up as quickly as possible. First scrape off anything solid with a knife. Blot up the liquid with paper towels.

Washable items: Soak in biological detergent for as long as possible, then rinse thoroughly. If the stain remains, then treat with liquid detergent in warm water with 5 ml (1 teaspoonful) of 20 vol. hydrogen peroxide per 600 ml (1 pint) stirred into the solution. Rinse well, then wash the item as usual.

Non-washable items: Blot or scrape as much as possible, take to the dry cleaner.

Furnishings, carpets: Sponge with lukewarm, clean water. Blot the stain dry, then use a proprietary pet stain remover. On carpets, use diluted carpet shampoo first. Don't let the pile get too wet. If the stain persists, then loosen it with a solution of 1 part white distilled vinegar to 3 parts water, blot dry.

ANTI-PERSPIRANTS

Washable items: Apply a paste of bicarbonate of soda and salt to the area and leave for a quarter of an hour, then soak in biological detergent and wash in the usual way.

Non-washable items: Treat with bicarbonate of soda and salt as above, then take to the dry cleaner.

BALLPOINT PENS

Washable items: Soak spot in methylated spirit, then soak in biological detergent, rinse.

Non-washable items: Treat with methylated spirit if the mark is small, otherwise take to the dry cleaner.

BEERS, ALES AND STOUTS

Washable items: Soak in biological washing powder, then wash.

Non-washable items: Blot up as much as possible with a piece of kitchen paper or a paper handkerchief, dab with white vinegar, then blot again.

BEETROOT

Washable items: Soak immediately in cold water, leave for as long as possible, rub liquid detergent into the mark, unless the fabric is woollen. If this does not remove it, soak in biological detergent, sprinkle borax on the stain, pour over boiling water, then wash in the usual way.

149

Non-washable items: Sponge with cold water to lessen the stain then take to a dry cleaner.

Furnishings, carpets: Treat furnishings as for non-washable items. Sponge carpet with cold water, blot and shampoo.

BIRD DROPPINGS

Washable items: Scrape off the surface of the fabric and soak in a biological powder before washing as usual. If there are coloured stains (due to a bird's diet of berries) you may have to bleach white cottons to remove all traces.

Non-washable items: Scrape off the worst; make up a solution of 1 part ammonia to 6 parts water and sponge this into the stain, but do a test first on coloured fabrics. Blot off any excess moisture and finish by dabbing with vinegar.

Furnishings, carpets: Scrape up anything that is on the surface then wipe clean with warm water or use a proprietary dry cleaning spray.

BLOOD

Washable items: Soak immediately in strongly salted cold water. Keep changing the salt water solution until it runs clear, rub any remaining marks with a salt paste. If the stain is obstinate, try saliva for small spots (spit on to some cotton wool) or meat tenderizer. Then soak in biological detergent and wash in the normal way. Be sure all the stain has gone before you do this as the slightest heat will seal in the mark. If the stain is old, try loosening it overnight with a cool solution of biological detergent. In the case of wool fabrics, if possible, leave under a cold running tap so the water runs through the material. This will prevent it felting which is a danger if you rub the stain. Try this solution for obstinate blood stains: soak in a solution of 10 ml (2 teaspoons) of household ammonia to half a litre (1 pint) of water and a few drops of hydrogen peroxide. Follow by a wash in biological detergent.

Non-washable items: Sponge the spot using cold water with a few drops of ammonia in it. Rinse with cold water and blot dry. Take to a dry cleaner if necessary.

Furnishings, carpets: Small stains on upholstery can be tackled with a paste of cornflour and salt. Allow it to dry, then brush off. Repeat if necessary. Place the object in the sun to dry if possible as this will help the cornflour to absorb the blood. Blankets should be soaked in cold salt water, then washed in biological detergent. For treatment of blood-stained mattresses, see page 146. Blood on carpets should be soaked out with cold water, blotted with paper tissues or kitchen towels until clear, then the carpet should be shampooed.

Dried stains: Soak washables (silk and wool excepted) overnight in a biological powder and water solution. For non-washables, dampen with lemon juice, sprinkle with salt, then iron between two sheets of dampened blotting paper.

BUTTER, MARGARINE, FATS

Washable items: Take off as much of the surface deposit as possible, then treat with a proprietary grease solvent. The article should then be washed at the highest temperature that the material can stand.

Non-washable items: Use a proprietary grease solvent, preferably an aerosol one. If the stain is very big, then it will be necessary to take the articles to the dry cleaner.

Furnishings, carpets: Treat as for non-washable items, in the case of carpets, follow up with a dry carpet cleaner.

CANDLE WAX

Washable items: If possible put the article in the freezer to harden it. The pieces then break off easily. If any wax is left, put the fabric between two clean pieces of blotting paper or towelling and press with a warm iron. Use a low setting to melt the wax, which should be absorbed by the paper underneath. Shift the paper to a clean patch and continue until no more wax appears. Use methylated spirit to get rid of any residual colour.

Non-washable items: Use the freezer method, then the iron, then dry cleaning fluid.

Furniture, furnishings and carpets: Wax on a wooden table top should be chilled first with a bagful of ice cubes, then gently scraped off, finally rubbed away with a hot clean cloth. Or, try washing it down with a solution of water and vinegar. Furnishings should be treated as non-washable fabrics. Carpets should have the wax picked off gently from the pile (chill first with ice cubes) then melted with a warm iron on blotting paper. Rub with methylated spirit, then sponge with diluted carpet shampoo and rinse.

CAR WAX AND POLISH

Blot all items with dry cleaning fluid, then liquid detergent, then rinse.

CARBON PAPER

Washable items: Rub with undiluted liquid detergent, then rinse well. If this doesn't work, then add a few drops of ammonia to the solution and try again.

Non-washable items: Dab with methylated spirit or white spirit (this method can be used for washable fabrics, too). On acetate or rayon, use a proprietary stain remover only, or take to the dry cleaner.

CHEWING GUM

Washable items: Get off as much as possible, then place the garment in a plastic bag in the freezer for an hour or so, when the gum should break off easily. Any residue can be removed by covering with brown paper and ironing.

Non-washable items: Freeze as above, then treat any marks left over with methylated or white spirit except for acetates or rayons. Then take to the dry cleaner if necessary.

Furnishings, carpets: Patient application of ice cubes to the spot may well harden chewing gum enough for it to be picked off. Follow up with methylated spirit to remove any traces left. Do not be tempted to use a vacuum cleaner on chewing gum in carpets, as it may gum up the works.

CHOCOLATE

Washable items: Scrape off as much as possible immediately, then dab with cool soapy water. If it is still marked, sponge with a warm borax solution – 25 g (1 oz) to 600 ml (1 pint) warm water. Another method is to sponge with warm water, sprinkle with dry borax, rub it in with your fingertips, leave for half an hour, rinse and launder.

Non-washable items: Scrape off as much as possible, use a grease solvent or take to the dry cleaner.

Furnishings, carpets: Scrape off as much as possible, but be careful not to damage the material, then use a dilute solution of upholstery or carpet shampoo.

COCOA

Washable items: Saturate the material with cool water, then soak in warm biological detergent. If this fails, then try a borax solution, as with chocolate (see above).

Non-washable items: Try using a grease solvent or take to the dry cleaner.

Furnishings, carpets: For furnishings, sponge with cool water and detergent or use upholstery shampoo. Use carpet shampoo on carpets or rub with glycerine and warm water in equal parts for really stubborn stains. Leave the mix on for some time then rinse off.

COD LIVER OIL

Washable items: Scoop up as much as you can, treat with cleaning solvent from the back of the fabric, then wash in strong detergent. Act quickly, as old cod liver oil stains are almost impossible to remove.

Non-washable items: Treat with cleaning solvent from the back.

Furnishings, carpets: Treat with cleaning solvent.

COFFEE

Washable items: Soak in a biological detergent in hand hot water and leave overnight. If you want immediate results, then sponge with a cloth dipped in a warm water and borax solution – 25 g (1 oz) to 600 ml (1 pint).

Non-washable items: Sponge with borax solution, blot with a tissue and any traces left can be dabbed lightly with a proprietary grease solvent.

Furnishings, carpets: Sponge with clear water and blot well, then treat with cleaning solvent. Shampoo carpets with a warm solution of carpet shampoo. Allow to dry and vacuum. DO NOT SOAK. If the stain is old, then glycerine with equal parts of warm water may shift it if you leave it on for a while, then rinse carefully.

COLAS

Washable items: Rinse with cold water, work in liquid detergent from the back of the fabric and rinse. If the stain persists, try methylated spirit mixed with a little white vinegar and water, rinse well and wash.

Non-washable items and carpets: Dab with cold water, taking care not to saturate carpets then treat with methylated spirit and rinse well.

CRAYONS AND CHALKS

Washable items: Brush off any chalk or pieces of crayon, then sponge with detergent until the stain disappears. If the crayon is indelible, then use a cloth dipped in methylated spirit instead.

Non-washable items: Brush off what you can, then take to the dry cleaner.

Furnishings, carpets: Try methylated spirit on furnishings if the mark does not brush off. Chalks trodden into carpets can be brushed, then vacuumed out; crayon marks can be treated by covering the stain with blotting paper and ironing with a warm iron. Then clean the area with a little white spirit.

CREAM

Washable items: Scrape off as much as possible, then rinse in cold water first before soaking in a biological detergent. If necessary, follow up with dry cleaning fluid to remove the last of the grease.

Non-washable items: Scrape, treat with dry cleaning fluid. If this does not work, take to the dry cleaner.

Furnishings, carpets: Tackle with dry cleaning fluid, rinse well afterwards and blot dry. On carpets, use a dry cleaning solvent, followed by carpet shampoo.

CREOSOTE

Washable items: Sponge with eucalyptus oil, then wash.

Non-washable items: Take to the dry cleaner.

Furnishings, carpets: Take to the cleaners if possible. Otherwise rub the area with a pad soaked in eucalyptus oil. Be careful not to spread the stain and rinse well afterwards, then blot dry.

155

CURRY

Washable items: Dip into lukewarm water until it runs clear, soak in biological powder, then rinse as usual.

Non-washable items: Sponge with solution of borax and warm water. If the stain remains, send to the dry cleaner.

Furnishings, carpets: Treat furnishings as for non-washable items. Treat carpets with the borax solution of 15 ml (1 tablespoon) borax to 600 ml (1 pint) warm water. If the stain persists, use a half and half solution of glycerine and water. The carpet may have to be cleaned professionally if the stain is large.

DEODORANTS (see Antiperspirants)

DYE

Washable items: Splashes should be dabbed up immediately they are made. Small stains will usually respond to sponging with methylated spirit to which a few drops of ammonia have been added. But test first with coloured and rayons. Alternatively, try lots of cold water and a long soak in biological detergent. If all else fails, you can use a proprietary dye stripper on the entire garment.

Non-washable items: Take to the dry cleaner immediately.

Furnishings, carpets: Small splashes can sometimes be removed with methylated spirit on both furnishings and carpets. If a large area of the carpet is affected, it is best to call in a professional cleaner.

EGG

Washable items: A soak in biological detergent will usually remove egg stains. But if they look as though they have set, soak them first in cold water and then follow up with the biological detergent solution. You may need to follow up the treatment with a dry cleaning solvent.

Non-washable items: Try dabbing with washing-up liquid, followed by a grease solvent.

Furnishings, carpets: Scrape off any excess, then treat with grease solvent. Shampoo carpets.

FATS (see **Butter**)

FELT-TIP PENS

Washable items: Treat with methylated spirit unless the fabric is an acetate, then rub soap into the area and wash.

Non-washable items: Small spots can be tackled with methylated spirit, otherwise take to the dry cleaner.

Furnishings, carpets: Treat fabrics as non-washable items. Plastic and leather should be tackled with a non-abrasive household cleaner if methylated spirit is not effective – wrap a finger in a piece of clean rag and apply to the area.

FRUIT STAINS

Washable items: Rinse immediately in cold water until no more colour comes out, then stretch the fabric over a bowl or pudding basin (use an elastic band or piece of string to keep it in place) then pour boiling water over the area from a kettle. The more force you do this with, the better. So, hold the kettle as high as possible. If the stain is shifting easily, then wash the garment at the highest temperature the fabric will stand (check the label first). If the stain is stubborn, then soak in 1 part 20 vol. hydrogen peroxide to 6 parts water – but be sure the material is colourfast first. Or use a proprietary stain remover. Acetate fabrics should be soaked in borax – 15 ml (1 tablespoon) to $\frac{1}{2}$ litre (1 pint).

Non-washable items: Sponge with cold water, then with glycerine. Leave for an hour, then sponge with white vinegar. Finish by sponging with a clean damp cloth.

Furnishings, carpets: Follow the advice for non-washable fabrics on furnishings. Blot up the stain on carpets with kitchen paper towelling, sponge with cold water, then shampoo the area with carpet shampoo. If any stain remains, try methylated spirit.

Fruit stained fingers: These can be cleaned up with a cotton wool pad soaked in nail varnish remover.

FURNITURE POLISH

Washable items: Treat with a dry cleaning solvent, then wash in the usual way.

Non-washable items: Try dry cleaning solvent, otherwise take to dry cleaner.

Furnishings, carpets: Treat with dry cleaning solvent, then follow up with upholstery or carpet shampoo.

GRASS

Washable items: Treat the affected area with methylated spirit unless the fabric is acetate, when you should use a proprietary stain remover, rinse, then wash normally.

Non-washable items: Apply a paste made of equal quantities of salt and cream of tartar, plus a little water, to the area. Leave it to dry then brush out. Use a proprietary stain remover if a mark remains or send to the dry cleaner.

GRAVY

Washable items: The staining ingredient in gravy is often grease-based, so plunge the area into cold water first, then treat with dry cleaning fluid before washing in hot water.

Non-washable items: These can be dabbed gently with soapy water. Blot dry, then use a solvent.

Furnishings, carpets: Try dry cleaning fluid first, then follow up with upholstery or carpet shampoo.

GREASE

Washable items: If the stain is newly made, scrape, then pat talcum powder, Fuller's earth or cornflour into it to absorb as much of the grease as possible, then brush off and remove the rest with dry cleaning solvent sponging on the *wrong* side. Finally, wash in hot water.

Non-washable items: Scrape off the excess, pat in talcum powder as above, then use a spray dry cleaning solvent. Otherwise take to a dry cleaner.

Furnishings, carpets: Treat furnishings as for non-washable items. On carpets, blot up as much grease as possible with absorbent paper towelling, then sprinkle with talcum powder, Fuller's earth or cornflour. Leave to absorb the grease and then vacuum. If the stain is still there, use a dry carpet shampoo. Grease marks on wallpaper can sometimes be removed by pressing a paste of Fuller's earth to the wall. Brush off when dry and repeat if the stain is still there.

HAIR COLOURANTS

Washable items: Tackle immediately, once the stain has dried it is almost impossible to remove. Soak in cold water, rub with liquid detergent, then with white distilled vinegar, then soak in biological detergent if the stain persists. Henna stains respond to treatment with neat household ammonia or if the marks are stubborn tackle them with methylated spirit. Light coloured garments can be left for a while in a mix of 1 part 20 vol. hydrogen peroxide to 6 parts water. Rinse well afterwards.

Non-washable items: Rub with liquid detergent, rinse. Take to the dry cleaner if the mark persists.

Furnishings, carpets: Dab with cold water, then rub with liquid detergent and blot dry. Professional help may be needed if the mark does not come out.

ICE CREAM

Washable items: Scrape off the excess with a blunt-edged knife, soak in a biological detergent, then, if a mark still remains, use a dry cleaning fluid to remove the rest. Dried on stains can be treated with a solution of 15 ml (1 tablespoon) of borax to 600 ml (1 pint) of warm water.

Non-washable items: Treat the stain with a grease solvent then, if necessary, take to the dry cleaner.

Furnishings, carpets: Furnishings should be treated as non-washable items. Treat carpets first with a grease solvent then follow up with a diluted carpet shampoo.

INK

Washable items: For ball point stains, see page 149. For fountain pen ink, apply liquid detergent immediately. In the case of stubborn stains on white cotton or linen, rub with lemon dipped in salt, then pour boiling water through the fabric. If this fails you can try a bleach solution (follow the manufacturer's instructions).

Non-washable items: Try dabbing felt tip, printer's ink or typewriter ribbon stains with methylated spirit. Otherwise take to a dry cleaner.

Furnishings, carpets: Blot, then treat with methylated spirit on a clean cloth. Be careful not to soak carpets. Fountain pen ink may respond to treatment with a detergent solution or carpet shampoo. Dried ink stains may need professional treatment and some stains will be permanent.

IODINE

Washable items: Remove brown stain with hypo crystals – used in photography – 15 ml (1 tablespoon) dissolved in 450 ml ($\frac{3}{4}$ pint) water. Soak stain in the solution for ten minutes, rinse and wash.

Non-washable items: Try treating with methylated spirit, if this fails, take to the dry cleaner.

Furnishings, carpets: Blot, then sponge with methylated spirit. Rinse well.

IRON-MOULD

Washable items: Light stains can be removed by rubbing lemon juice and salt into the mark. Leave for about an hour, then rinse well. Repeat if necessary. If the stain does not shift, use a proprietary iron-mould or dye remover or a solution of oxalic acid: 5 ml (1 teaspoon) in a litre (2 pints) of water but be careful as the acid is extremely poisonous. Do not use on silks and woollens.

Non-washable items: Take straight to the dry cleaner.

Furnishings: Try the salt and lemon treatment or try a proprietary remover. If this fails, get professional help.

JAMS, MARMALADE, HONEY, ETC.

Washable items: Scrape, soak in biological detergent and then wash in the usual way. If the stain persists, soak in a solution of 15 ml (1 tablespoon) of borax to 600 ml (1 pint) of warm water, then rinse and wash in the usual way, OR, use a solution of 1 part 20 vol. hydrogen peroxide to 6 parts water, rinse well.

Non-washable items: Scrape, rinse in cold soapy water. If a mark remains, rub in a little borax, leave for a minute or two, then sponge. If still stained, take to a dry cleaner.

161

Furnishing, carpets: Scrape off excess, sponge with warm water, then treat with upholstery or carpet shampoo.

KETCHUP, PICKLES, ETC.

Washable items: Scrape off excess, rinse thoroughly in cold water, then sponge with warm water and liquid detergent and, if the fabric is colourfast, soak in 1 part 20 vol. hydrogen peroxide to 6 parts water, rinse and dry. If a mark remains, try using methylated spirit.

Non-washable items: Scrape, sponge with cold water, blot, then try an aerosol stain remover. Tomato sauce stains may need the attention of a professional dry cleaner.

Furnishings, carpets: Scrape, sponge with cold water, blot. Then try upholstery or carpet shampoo. If the stain persists, try rubbing a little glycerine into it to loosen it, then shampoo again and rinse.

LIPSTICK

Washable items: Sponge with methylated spirit, then dab with washing-up liquid (neat) and rinse through. For severe stains, rub in petroleum jelly to loosen, leave for a few minutes, dab with ammonia, then rinse.

Non-washable items: Use a proprietary dry cleaner.

Furnishings, carpets: Scrape off excess, treat with proprietary dry cleaning solvent, then use upholstery or carpet shampoo.

MAKE-UP

Washable items: Remove any excess with a knife. Then pat with talcum powder to mop up any grease. Treat light stains with detergent and warm water, soak heavier ones in a solution of 5 ml (1 teaspoon) of ammonia to 600 ml (1 pint) lukewarm water or treat with a dry cleaning solvent.

Non-washable items: Scrape off any excess, pat in talcum powder to absorb grease, then use an aerosol dry cleaning solvent or methylated spirit.

Furnishings, carpets: Scrape off excess, use techniques described for non-washable items. Follow up with upholstery or carpet shampoo.

MARGARINE (see **Butter**)

MARMALADE (see **Jams**)

MASCARA

Washable items: Rub in neat washing-up liquid, then wash as usual. If this does not completely remove the stain, treat with a dry cleaning fluid.

Non-washable items: If colourfast, treat with methylated spirit. Otherwise use aerosol stain remover and if a mark persists, blot with 1 part ammonia diluted in 3 parts cold water, on colourfast fabrics only. Rinse.

Furnishings, carpets: Tackle as for non-washable items.

MAYONNAISE

Washable items: Scrape off excess, then treat with a proprietary grease solvent. Soak in a solution of biological detergent and water according to the packet instructions, then wash in lukewarm water only. If a mark remains, continue to treat with grease solvent.

Non-washable items: Remove as much as possible with a warm damp cloth, treat with grease solvent. If a mark remains, take to the dry cleaner.

Furnishings, carpets: Blot off as much as possible, then spray with aerosol stain remover, finally wash with upholstery or carpet shampoo.

MEDICINE

Washable items: Soak immediately in cold water, then wash. If a mark remains, remove it with methylated spirit.

Non-washable items: Take to a dry cleaner.

Furnishings, carpets: Blot with kitchen towelling, then rinse several times with cold water, blotting between each application. If a mark persists finish up with upholstery or carpet shampoo.

METAL POLISH

Washable items: Blot, to remove as much moisture as possible, then treat with white spirit or proprietary dry cleaner. Brush lightly when dry.

Non-washable items: Blot with a cloth moistened in proprietary dry cleaning solvent, then use an aerosol dry cleaner. If a stain persists, take to the dry cleaner.

Furnishing, carpets: Blot excess moisture, then treat with white spirit. Allow to dry then vacuum. If a mark remains, treat with upholstery or carpet shampoo.

MILDEW

Washable items: If tackled in time, ordinary laundering may remove the marks: rub well with washing soap beforehand. Otherwise, soak white cottons and linens in a weak solution of 15 ml (1 tablespoon) bleach to just over a litre (2 pints) of water plus 5 ml (1 teaspoon) of white distilled vinegar. Other fabrics can be soaked in 1 part 20 vol. hydrogen peroxide to 6 parts of water, but watch for possible bleeding of colour.

Non-washable items: Take to a dry cleaner.

Furnishings, carpets: Sponge with a mild solution of antiseptic. If this does not work, call in professional help. Mildew on books and paper should be wiped off with a soft cloth just moistened with mild antiseptic.

MILK

Washable items: Rinse in cold water, soak in biological detergent. For immediate results sponge with warm water and borax solution – 25 g (1 oz) to 600 ml (1 pint).

Non-washable items: Sponge with borax solution, blot with a tissue. Dab any remaining traces with grease solvent.

Furnishings, carpets: Blot well, then shampoo with a warm solution of carpet shampoo. Do not soak. Allow to dry, then vacuum.

MUD

Washable items: Allow the mud to dry and then brush off, working the fabric with a rubbing motion between your hands to remove as much as possible. Then wash in the usual way. If any marks remain, treat with proprietary dry cleaner and wash again.

Non-washable items: Leave to dry completely, then brush off. Sponge if necessary with detergent solution and follow up with aerosol dry cleaner.

Furnishings, carpets: Allow to dry, brush thoroughly and then vacuum. Use an upholstery or a carpet shampoo.

MUSTARD

Washable items: Sponge, then soak in liquid detergent before washing. If a stain remains, treat with a solution of 5 ml (1 teaspoon) of ammonia to 600 ml (1 pint) of water. Rinse.

165

Non-washable items: Spot treat, if possible, with mild detergent, then the ammonia solution above. If necessary, take to the dry cleaner.

Furnishings, carpets: Treat as for non-washable items. Dried-on stains on upholstery can be loosened with a solution of half and half glycerine and warm water.

NAIL VARNISH

Washable items: Blot as much as possible, then treat from the back of the fabric with amyl acetate, if you have some, failing that, *non-oily* nail varnish remover, then white spirit. Follow up, if necessary, with methylated spirit to clear the colour, but not on acetate fabrics.

Non-washable items: Take straight to a dry cleaner.

Furnishings, carpets: Blot, clean up with amyl acetate or *non-oily* nail varnish remover. Follow up with white spirit, then upholstery or carpet shampoo.

NEWSPRINT

Washable items: Sponge with methylated spirit, then wash.

Non-washable items: Sponge with methylated spirit, then cold water. If the stain remains, take to the dry cleaner.

Furnishings, carpets: Treat as for non-washable items.

ORANGE JUICE

Washable items: Soak immediately in cold water. If any stain remains, stretch the fabric over a bowl and pour hot water through the material.

Non-washable items: Sponge with cold water, then glycerine. Leave for an hour, then sponge with white vinegar. Finish with a damp cloth and leave to dry.

Furnishings, carpets: Sponge with cold water, then treat with upholstery or carpet shampoo and rinse.

PAINT, ACRYLIC

Washable items: Blot immediately and wash out as fast as possible with soap and cold water. If the paint has almost dried, scrape off what you can, then try proprietary dry cleaning fluid, methylated spirit or paint removing solvent. Acrylic paint that has dried on a garment is almost impossible to remove.

Non-washable items: Keep the stain damp, scrape off what you can and take to a dry cleaner as fast as possible.

Furnishings, carpets: Almost impossible to remove unless you tackle it while still damp. Scrape or blot, treat with upholstery or carpet shampoo and warm water, then try methylated spirit or paint removing solvent.

PAINT, CELLULOSE

Washable items: Treat immediately with cellulose thinners, then wash in the usual way.

Non-washable items: Take immediately to the dry cleaner.

Furnishings, carpets: Spot treat with cellulose thinners. Then use upholstery or carpet shampoo. If the patch is a large one, call in professional help.

PAINT, EMULSION

Washable items: Scrape or wipe off any excess as soon as it happens, then flood with cold water immediately, rinse until all traces of the paint have gone. Then wash in the usual way, finally use a grease solvent.

Non-washable items: Keep damp, scrape or blot then take to the dry cleaner as fast as possible.

Furnishings, carpets: Tackle immediately with plenty of cold water, then follow up with carpet or upholstery shampoo and, if necessary, grease solvent.

PAINT, ENAMEL

Washable items: Treat with a paint remover and a clean cloth, keep treating until the stain has gone, working from the front and back of the fabric. Then wash in the usual way, but do not immerse in water until you are satisfied the stain has gone.

Non-washable items: Take to a dry cleaner immediately.

Furnishings, carpets: Blot as much as possible then treat with dry cleaning fluid or paint remover.

PAINT, GLOSS

Washable items: Treat immediately with turpentine or white spirit or brush cleaner except on acetate fabrics. Sponge carefully with cold water then wash in the usual way. If necessary, follow up with proprietary stain remover.

Non-washable items: Treat with turpentine, white spirit or brush cleaner, except on acetate and rayon fabrics. If necessary, take to a dry cleaner.

Furnishings, carpets: Treat with white spirit or brush cleaner, then follow up with upholstery or carpet shampoo.

PAINT, OIL

Washable items: Flood immediately with white spirit (hold a pad of clean white cloth under the stain), then use a proprietary stain remover, if necessary. Wash in the normal way.

Non-washable items: Take to the dry cleaner immediately.

Furnishings, carpets: Clean up with white spirit, then use a stain remover if necessary, finish up with upholstery or carpet shampoo.

PAINT, WATER COLOUR

Washable items: Rinse well in cold water, if a stain persists, treat with a little neat ammonia. Rinse carefully.

Non-washable items: Try sponging with cold water, if this fails, take to a dry cleaner.

Furnishings, carpets: Sponge with cold water, then spot treat with neat ammonia if necessary, follow up with upholstery or carpet shampoo.

PARAFFIN

(N.B. This stain is highly inflammable)
Washable items: Scrape off any excess, then pat talcum powder, Fuller's earth or cornflour into the patch to absorb as much of the grease as possible. Finally, use a dry cleaning solvent and wash.

Non-washable items: Pat talcum powder, Fuller's earth or cornflour into the patch and try treating with a dry cleaning solvent. Larger areas can be treated by placing between two sheets of blotting paper and pressing with a warm iron (see Candlewax, page 151). Follow up with dry cleaning solvent. If this fails, send to a dry cleaner.

Furnishings, carpets: Blot the patch, apply aerosol stain remover. Treat large areas by placing a piece of blotting paper on top and pressing with a warm iron, then apply stain remover and shampoo.

PERFUME

Washable items: Rinse out immediately in lukewarm water, if a stain persists, treat with neat ammonia, then wash in the usual way. For dried-on perfume, rub a solution of equal parts glycerine and warm water into it, then wash.

Non-washable items: Rub a half-and-half glycerine and warm water solution into the stain, then sponge over carefully with a cloth wrung out in warm water. Precious fabrics should go straight to a dry cleaner.

Furnishings, carpets: Loosen the stain with a half-and-half mix of glycerine and warm water, then sponge carefully with a cloth wrung out in warm water. Blot well, follow up with upholstery or carpet shampoo if necessary.

PERSPIRATION

Washable items: Soak in biological detergent (follow packet instructions) and if the stain persists, treat with a weak solution of ammonia, rinse and then wash. Another trick is two aspirins dissolved in the rinsing water.

Non-washable items: Sponge with a solution of 1 teaspoon white vinegar to 250 ml (8 fl oz) warm water.

PETROLEUM JELLY

Washable items: Scrape off as much as possible, then wash in the hottest water the fabric will stand, adding plenty of detergent. If a stain remains, use a dry cleaning solvent.

Non-washable items: Scrape, use a dry cleaning solvent and, if a stain remains, take to a dry cleaner.

Furnishings, carpets: Scrape off as much as possible, then treat with a grease solvent, follow up with diluted upholstery or carpet shampoo, rinse and blot.

PLASTICINE

Washable items: Scrape off as much as possible, then tackle with a grease solvent or, failing that, a little lighter fuel on a piece of clean cloth. If the fabric is a man-made fibre, check first, on the inside of a pocket or of a seam, to make sure no damage is caused. Wash in the hottest possible water that the fabric will take.

Non-washable items: Scrape, spot treat with a grease solvent. If this does not work, then take to a dry cleaner for professional attention.

Furnishings, carpets: Furnishings should be treated as non-washable items. Plasticine trodden into the carpet should be scraped off, then the area treated with grease solvent. Follow up with carpet shampoo, rinse well. If a stain remains, allow the carpet to dry, then try methylated spirit.

PUTTY

Washable items: Chill in a fridge or freezer first, then pick off the excess and treat with dry cleaning fluid. Wash in the hottest possible water that the fabric will stand.

Non-washable items: Chill in a fridge or freezer if possible, then pick off surface putty, spot treat the stain with dry cleaning fluid. If necessary take to a dry cleaner.

Furnishings, carpets: Scrape off excess, then treat with dry cleaning solvent and follow up with upholstery or carpet shampoo.

SALAD DRESSING

Washable items: Blot, treat with an aerosol grease solvent, then wash in the hottest water that the fabric will take.

Non-washable items: Blot, spot treat with an aerosol grease solvent. If necessary, take to a dry cleaner.

Furnishings, carpets: Mop up as much of the excess as possible, then treat with an aerosol dry cleaner. Follow up, if necessary, with upholstery or carpet shampoo.

SCORCH MARKS

Washable items: Light marks will disappear if you soak the fabric in cold milk. Any traces should be dabbed with a solution of soapy water with 1 teaspoon of borax added, then rinsed. Any marks that remain on white cottons or linens can usually be bleached out.

Non-washable items: Sponge with the borax solution as above, rinse, blot dry.

Furnishings, carpets: Treat upholstery as for non-washable items. Scorch marks on carpets can sometimes be removed by sponging with 1 part 20 vol. hydrogen peroxide to 10 parts of water. Failing that, snip off the affected tufts if possible, or rub them over with fine wire wool, using a circular movement.

SHOE POLISH

Washable items: Scrape off excess. Tackle with white spirit or, if the stain is bad and the fabric sturdy, with paint brush cleaner. Small marks can often be removed with an aerosol grease solvent. Wash with detergent and hot water with a little ammonia added.

Non-washable items: Scrape, spot treat with aerosol dry cleaner. If this does not work, try white spirit or paint brush cleaner, failing that, get professional help.

Furnishings, carpets: Scrape off excess, tackle with white spirit, or methylated spirit and follow up with upholstery or carpet detergent.

SICK

Washable items: Take off as much as possible with a spoon. Rinse well under a cold tap, then soak in biological detergent – add disinfectant if necessary. Wash in the usual way. If any mark remains, and the fabric can take it (see pages 118–137), soak again in a mixture of 1 part 20 vol. hydrogen peroxide to 6 parts water.

Non-washable items: Scrape, try sponging with a little ammonia in warm water. If this does not work, take to a dry cleaner.

Furnishings, carpets: Scrape, sponge with warm water and detergent with a little disinfectant added. Carpets should be sprayed with a soda syphon first, if you have one to hand, then tackled with carpet shampoo. Mattresses should be sponged well with warm water and detergent, then rinsed in cold water with a little disinfectant added.

SOOT, SMOKE

Washable items: Tackle the marks with an aerosol dry cleaner, then wash.

Non-washable items: Use an aerosol dry cleaner, if this fails, get professional help.

Furnishings, carpets: Vacuum thoroughly, or shake, then use an aerosol stain remover. Alternatively, on light coloured carpets, rub in Fuller's earth, then vacuum again.

SPIRITS

Washable items: Sponge with warm water, then wash in the usual way.

Non-washable items: Spot treat with warm water and a little liquid detergent, then sponge with clear warm water and blot.

Furnishings, carpets: Sponge over with warm water then follow up with carpet or upholstery shampoo if necessary.

STOUTS (see Beers)

TAR

Washable items: Scrape off as much as you can, soften with a little glycerine, then remove the rest with eucalyptus oil, working from the back of the fabric. Small marks can often be removed with a dry cleaning solvent. Finally wash in the hottest possible temperature that the fabric will stand. Any stain that remains can usually be removed with a paint brush solvent.

Non-washable items: Scrape, soften with a little glycerine, rub gently with lighter fuel, then dab with a cloth wrung out in warm water.

Furnishings, carpets: Scrape, soften with glycerine, then use a grease solvent, or eucalyptus oil. Dark marks will usually come out with a paint brush solvent. Finish up with an upholstery or carpet shampoo.

TEA

Washable items: Soak in warm water with a little borax added, 15 ml (1 tablespoon) to 500 ml (1 pint) of water, then soak again in a biological detergent and wash as usual. Dried-on stains should be softened before treatment with a solution of equal amounts of glycerine and warm water. If a stain remains, after washing, try methylated spirit. It may be necessary to bleach cottons to remove all the stain.

Non-washable items: Treat with a solution of 15 ml (1 tablespoon) of borax to 600 ml (1 pint) of water, follow up with an aerosol stain remover.

Furnishings, carpets: Treat with a solution of 15 ml (1 tablespoon) of borax to 600 ml (1 pint) of water, follow up with an aerosol stain remover.

Cups and mugs: Tea-stained cups and mugs can be cleaned with a damp cloth dipped in bicarbonate of soda or soaked in a weak solution of bleach. Rinse thoroughly.

TOBACCO

Washable items: Treat the stain with methylated spirit, or if the fabric is acetate, benzine. Failing that, a solution of equal parts of hydrogen peroxide 20 vol. and water may remove the mark. Rinse well afterwards.

Non-washable items: Take to the dry cleaner.

Furnishings, carpets: Sponge with methylated spirit, then rinse and finish up with carpet or upholstery shampoo.

Tobacco-stained fingers: These can be cleaned up with the sterilizing fluid that is used for nappies or babies' bottles.

URINE

Washable items: Rinse well in cold water, then soak in biological detergent and launder in the usual way. Old stains, which can be difficult to remove, may be improved if you soak the garment in a mix of 1 part 20 vol. hydrogen peroxide to 6 parts of water with a few drops of household ammonia added.

Non-washable items: Sponge with cold water, then with a solution of 10 ml (2 teaspoons) of distilled white vinegar to 1 litre (2 pints) of water. If this fails, take to a dry cleaner.

Furnishings, carpets: Treat quickly, use plenty of clear water, washing and mopping up as you go to make sure the carpet does not become too wet. Finally shampoo.

VARNISH (SHELLAC)

Washable items: Wipe immediately with methylated spirit unless the fabric is acetate, wash in detergent and rinse.

Non-washable items: Tackle immediately with methylated spirit (not on acetate fabrics). If the stain remains take to dry cleaner.

Furnishings, carpets: Treat as for non-washable items.

WAX POLISH

Washable items: Treat with dry cleaning solvent, then wash in hot liquid detergent solution and rinse.

Non-washable items: Treat with dry cleaning solvent, sponge with warm detergent solution and rinse.

Furnishings, carpets: Treat as for non-washable items.

WINE

Washable items: Pour salt on to the stain to blot it, then soak in cold water and rinse. If a mark remains, stretch the area over a basin, sprinkle on borax and pour over boiling water.

Non-washable items: Sponge with warm water and blot with blotting paper. Sprinkle with talcum powder to absorb the stain for an hour, sponge again and blot.

Furnishings, carpets: Blot up as much as possible, then rinse and blot the area. In the case of carpets, do not let them become too wet; finish with a carpet shampoo.

Some handy home-made solutions

Oven cleaner: Ammonia makes an inexpensive oven cleaner but it can burn the skin, so wear rubber gloves and handle it carefully.

Stain remover: Bicarbonate of soda and water paste makes a good emergency treatment on washable items (not furnishings) for fruit, tea or coffee stains. Rub on, leave for half an hour, then sponge off.

Improved polish: Cider vinegar, 5 ml (1 teaspoonful) added to a cupful of liquid furniture polish, makes it go on more smoothly, improves its performance.

Window cleaner: Cold wash detergent, diluted 1 capful to 1 litre (2 pints) of cold water, makes a good window cleaner.

Glass polisher: Crumpled newspaper gives windows and glass items a polish after they have been washed.

Bottom of the oven cleaner: Dishwasher powder will clean up burned-on food in the bottom of ovens. Wait until the oven has cooled, sprinkle on the offending spot, cover with a damp paper towel and leave overnight. Wash off with warm water in the morning.

Metal and china stain remover: Wood ash used as a scourer, will take some stains off metal and china objects.

Marble top polish: A lemon slice wrapped in a strip of clean cloth, dipped in borax will make marble table tops shine.

Furniture polish: Linseed oil, 2 parts to 1 part of turpentine and 1 part of water makes a good furniture polish.

Upholstery cleaner: Liquid detergent and boiling water mixed at a ratio of 1:4, will cool to make a jelly. Whip it up with an egg beater and it makes a good foam for cleaning upholstery.

Flannel rinse: Malt vinegar and water as a rinse will get soap out of face flannels. Use 10 ml (2 teaspoons) of vinegar to 600 ml (1 pint) of water. Combined with a few grains of uncooked rice, it will clean out a narrow necked bottle.

Chrome and paintwork cleaner: 2 parts paraffin, mixed with 1 part methylated spirit makes a good polish for chrome and paintwork.

Drain cleaner: Salt in a solution of hot water, will help to clear drains and gets rid of an unpleasant smell. Use 15 ml of salt to 600 ml of water (a tablespoon to a pint).

Emergency upholstery cleaner: Shaving cream in an aerosol can is another good emergency upholstery cleaner. Use it in exactly the same way as upholstery foam.

First class furniture polish: Turpentine, vinegar and boiling water mixed in equal parts, make a good furniture polish.

Wall cleaner: $\frac{1}{4}$ cup of washing soda, combined with $\frac{1}{2}$ cup of ammonia and $\frac{1}{4}$ cup white distilled vinegar, added to a bucket of warm water, make a good solution for sponging down grimy walls.

Tiled floor cleaner: One cup of distilled white vinegar in a pail of water makes a rinse for linoleum or PVC tiled floors, leaves them sparkling.

Floor mop rinse: Fabric softener, a capful added to a pail of water, makes a good rinse for a cotton floor mop, leaves it soft and fluffy for the next time.

Stains
on household surfaces

ALUMINIUM COOKWARE

Burnt-on food should be removed by boiling some water in in the pan, then working on the softened deposit with a nylon brush or scourer. **Stains** can be removed by soaking the pan in a solution of 15 ml (1 tablespoonful) of borax to 600 ml (1 pint) of water. **Tide marks** left by hard water when it is boiled can be removed with lemon. Boil up some pieces of lemon peel in the saucepan, making sure the water level comes above the tide mark. The same effect can be achieved by boiling up apples or rhubarb in the pan. **Bad stains** can often be removed by simmering a strong solution of vinegar in the pan for about 15 minutes. Use 3 parts of vinegar to 1 part of water. **Surface pitting** will often occur if food is left in aluminium pans overnight, so transfer it to another container. When removing stains with steel wool, rub in one direction only to avoid scratch marks and make sure that you rinse the pan out well afterwards. Roasting tins can be treated in the same way.

BATHS, ACRYLIC

Surface scratches can be buffed out with a little silver metal polish on a clean rag. **Light stains** can be rubbed with some liquid detergent on a soft cloth. **Bad scratches or stains** should be rubbed cautiously with 'wet and dry' sandpaper, used damp. Use the same piece of sandpaper until it is worn right down, follow up with silver metal polish. You could also try a proprietary gently abrasive liquid cleaner on the stubborn stains. Do not try these techniques on glass fibre baths, ask the manufacturer's advice.

BATHS, CAST IRON, PRESSED STEEL

Yellow marks and discoloration can sometimes be removed with a wedge of lemon dipped in coarse salt. Rinse well, or the acid in the lemon may take the shine off the surface. For tougher cases, try a salt and turpentine paste rubbed well in. For other marks there are good proprietary cleaners that will do a good cleaning job, but follow the manufacturer's instructions carefully: left on too long, they can eat into the enamel or porcelain surface. **Tide marks** that won't respond to normal cleaning techniques can be rubbed off with white spirit, then rinsed with a solution of washing-up liquid and warm water. (See also page 80 for tips on everyday care of the bath.)

BRASS

Badly tarnished brass can be cleaned with a lemon dipped in salt, or a paste of vinegar, flour and salt in equal quantities. Both these mixtures must be washed off and the brass rinsed to prevent it affecting the metal but they are worth trying, as they are cheap and effective.

BRONZE

Green spots on bronze should be rubbed over with turpentine. Allow to dry, brush with a dry nailbrush, then apply a little oil to the surface and polish. Lacquered bronze sometimes cracks and peels but in this case it will have to be treated professionally.

CAST-IRON COOKWARE

Burnt-on food should come off if you boil up a solution of water with a few crystals of washing soda added. The pan must be dried immediately or it will tend to rust. If this happens, clean off with fine steel wool and rinse well. Dry thoroughly, then rub a little cooking oil into the surface before storing, to prevent further rusting.

CERAMIC TILES

Rust stains left by metal objects can be cleaned off with abrasive cleaning powder. **Lime stains** should be rubbed with neat white distilled vinegar. Leave on for ten minutes then rinse off. **Soap marks** can be rubbed off with paraffin. **Mild stains** can be removed with a solution of 1 cup ammonia, 1 cup white distilled vinegar to a bucket of warm water with a few washing soda crystals added. **Grouting blackened with mildew** can be cleaned using an old toothbrush and a half household bleach, half water solution. Take care though: wear rubber gloves and protect the bath with thick wads of newspaper. Stand well back to avoid splashes and work with the window open, rinsing as you go.

COOKERS, ELECTRIC

First turn off the electricity supply at the cooker point. **Burnt-on marks** on vitreous enamel surfaces should be tackled with a mild abrasive cleaning powder (make sure the mark is thoroughly moist first). Follow up, if necessary, with a special vitreous enamel cleaner. See **Ovens** for instructions on cleaning inside the cooker.

COOKERS, GAS

First turn off the pilot lights. Any removable parts should be soaked in hot detergent solution. Add a few crystals of washing soda in really bad cases, then clean up with steel wool. Rinse and dry thoroughly before replacing. See electric cookers, above, for other surfaces. Be sure to relight the pilot flames after cleaning. See **Ovens** for instructions on cleaning inside the cooker.

COPPER

Stains on the outside of copper saucepans can often be removed by a cloth dipped in vinegar, sprinkled with coarse salt. Follow up with a proprietary cleaner and polish. They will work better if you do not clean the base.

181

ENAMEL COOKWARE

Burnt-on food stains should be shifted by boiling up a solution of 10 ml (2 teaspoons) of bicarbonate of soda in a panful of water. Otherwise, soak the pan in washing-up liquid in hot water, then rub with a paste of bicarbonate of soda. **Residual stains** should go if you fill the pan with cold water and add 5 ml (1 teaspoonful) of bleach. Leave overnight and rinse well afterwards.

GLASS

Glass shelves and table tops can be cleaned by wiping with a mixture of vinegar and water, or use a window cleaner or general purpose spray cleaner. Stubborn **grease stains** can be wiped off with methylated spirit. Finish up with window-cleaning liquid and polish. Allow to dry, wipe off. **Stains on cut glass** should be rubbed off with a solution of 1 part vinegar to 3 parts warm water. **Interior stains** should be soaked in the vinegar solution for some hours, failing that, try using 1 part lemon juice to 3 parts distilled water. If the stain persists, pour in some coarse table salt, cover with vinegar and swill. If the glass has **discoloration** after long storage, soak, then wash in warm detergent with 15 ml (1 tablespoon) of ammonia added. Rinse well afterwards. Fine scratches can be removed by using a metal polish on wadding and rubbing in small circles.

IRONS, ELECTRIC

Melted synthetic or starch stains should be tackled while the iron is still warm, but unplugged. Scrape off any excess with a round-bladed knife covered with a piece of white cotton cloth. Then use a stick iron cleaner, following the manufacturer's instructions carefully. Use in a well-ventilated room as the process gives off fumes. For less major stains, one old-fashioned remedy is to warm the iron, unplug it, then run a bar of soap over the soleplate. Iron the soap off on to an old cloth. **Burn marks** will usually come off if you rub them with a hot salt and vinegar paste.

STAINS ON HOUSEHOLD SURFACES

IRONS, STEAM

Proceed as for electric irons, but hold the iron at an angle
while cleaning the soleplate so that any debris falls on to the
working top and not back into the steam vents, clogging
them. **Furring** inside steam irons can be removed with a
steam iron cleaner, available from chemists.

KETTLES

Furring and scale deposits: The vinegar treatment may
help with defurring but check first with the kettle manufacturer's instructions, as some materials and finishes will not
withstand it. See page 183 for the method to use. Otherwise
use a proprietary kettle descaler, following the manufacturer's instructions. Rinse well afterwards. To prevent
kettles furring up, pop an oyster shell inside to collect any
deposits.

LAMINATED PLASTIC SURFACES

Treat **difficult stains** with cream cleansers, or a little dry
bicarbonate of soda on a damp cloth. Tea stains and other
stubborn stains on white laminated plastic can be sponged off
with a mild bleach solution, 5 ml (1 teaspoon) of bleach to 600
ml (1 pint) of water, but rinse well immediately afterwards
and do not use on coloured or patterned surfaces as it will
damage.

LAVATORY

Avoid staining as much as possible by installing a proprietary flush deodorizer/cleaner in the cistern, which
contains detergent. Otherwise tackle stains with a proprietary lavatory cleaner but never mix two different
brands of powder or they may set up an unpleasant
chemical reaction. **Bad stains** can be tackled with a paste of
borax and lemon juice. Rub it on to the surface and leave
for several hours. Stains under the rim can be treated this
way, or use a proprietary lavatory cleaner.

LEATHER COVERED SURFACES

Be careful with special finishes on leather, follow the manufacturer's instructions for these. Some specialist companies sell special renovation kits for improving the appearance of old leather. If leather furniture in daily use becomes covered in finger marks, wipe with a cloth wrung out in water with a little vinegar added. Don't wet the leather, wring the cloth out well, and just wipe over the surface to pick up the grease. Leather desk tops can be treated with a squirt of washing-up liquid to 600 ml (1 pint) of water. Dip the cloth in the solution, wring out and wipe over the desk top.

MIRRORS

Remove **hair lacquer** stains with methylated spirit. **General stains** can be rubbed off with a mild solution of white distilled vinegar and warm water or ammonia and water. Use 5 ml (1 teaspoon) to 600 ml (1 pint) of water. Cold tea will also often remove marks on mirrors. If the stain persists, then treat it with a solution of 15 ml (1 tablespoon) of borax to 600 ml (1 pint) of water. Be careful not to wet the mirror backing. Otherwise it may cause spotting or make the 'silver' flake off.

NON-STICK COOKWARE

The black non-stick finishes in pans can be cleaned using a cup of bleach and 2 teaspoons of bicarbonate of soda. Three quarters fill the pan with hot water and boil this mixture for 10–15 minutes. It makes an awful smell, so open the window and leave the room. Then rinse and dry the pan before rubbing around the whole of the inside surface with a little oil.

OVENS

Self-cleaning models should keep themselves clean. Occasional wiping with a damp cloth and alternating roasting with medium to high temperature dry cooking (i.e. baking) is all that is needed. Otherwise follow the manufacturer's instructions. Unplug an electric cooker at the cooker point, turn off the pilot lights on a gas cooker, then wipe up **general stains** with a soft cloth and washing-up liquid solution while the oven is still warm after a cooking session. Take out oven shelves if necessary and soak in hot detergent, scrubbing bad stains with a nylon pot scourer. For **stubborn stains** use a proprietary aerosol or pad oven cleaner, following the manufacturer's instructions. Wear rubber gloves while cleaning and remember to protect the floor. **Stains on glass oven doors** should be removed by rubbing over with bicarbonate of soda or liquid bath cleaner while the door is still warm. Do not use aerosol cleaners on glass oven doors as they could lead to the glass shattering. A **microwave cooker** can be cleaned by standing a dish of hot water in it. Add a slice of lemon and boil the water in the oven until plenty of steam is produced, then wipe over the interior with a damp cloth. Put the **chrome rings** from a gas cooker in a plastic bag, add a large cup of ammonia, seal and leave for several hours. Rinse out of doors with a garden hose or throw a bucket of water over them.

SILVER

Heavily tarnished silver can be treated with aluminium foil and washing soda. Lay a strip of aluminium foil in a non-metal basin. Put the silver object on top of it, add a few crystals of washing soda, then cover with hot water. Leave for a few minutes then rinse. Otherwise use a proprietary silver cleaner, following the manufacturer's instructions. An impregnated silver cloth is useful to shine up silver quickly or to wrap around silver that is to be stored.

SINKS, ENAMEL

Light stains can usually be removed by rubbing with fresh lemon or a paste of lemon juice and borax. For **stubborn stains,** use a proprietary vitreous enamel cleaner. Do not use bleach unless you have to, for this will tend to make the sink look yellow. Do not use abrasive scouring pads as these will leave scratches.

SINKS, STAINLESS STEEL

General stains should come off if you rub them with neat detergent. **Rust stains** can be removed with mild cream bath cleaner or, failing that, rub with lighter fuel. **Water marks** can be removed by polishing off with methylated spirit on a soft cloth. Do not use steel wool as it may scratch the surface and spoil its appearance.

STAINLESS STEEL COOKWARE

Do not use metal scourers or scouring powders as these will scratch the surface. To remove **stubborn deposits,** soak in warm water. To **restore the appearance** of your pan, use either a proprietary stainless steel cleaner, or a mild culinary acid, such as lemon juice or vinegar. Apply with a cloth and wipe over the inside and outside of the pan.

STAINLESS STEEL CUTLERY

General stains should come off with a hot solution of detergent. Otherwise, try using a proprietary stainless steel polish on a soft cloth.

WALLPAPER

General stains can often be removed if you rub over the surface with a soft India rubber, or a ball of moistened white bread. **Candlewax and wax stains** should be softened carefully first with a hair dryer – do not allow them to get too hot, cover with blotting paper, then press with a warm iron. Finally, blot the remainder carefully with methylated spirit. **Crayon scribbles** on washable wallpapers can often be removed with dry cleaning fluid or by rubbing gently with a moist cloth sprinkled with bicarbonate of soda. **Grease stains** should be treated in the same way as wax, or tackled with dry cleaning fluid. All these treatments should be tested out first on a spare piece of wallpaper. If the stain will not come out and you have some paper to spare, tear out the wallpaper for the affected area in a jagged shape and patch. It will be less noticeable repaired that way than if you cut out a neat square. As a last resort, hang an ornament or picture over the spot.

WASHBASINS

Porcelain washbasins will keep their shining appearance if you rub them regularly with coarse salt. Prevent stains from forming by a daily wipe with a mild soap solution and beware of using stronger cleaners which may scratch the surface and make future cleaning more difficult. Hard water deposits around taps can be treated with lemon juice and salt (see page 91). If there is a build-up of **hard water deposits,** hang a plastic container full of water softener and water around the top so that the outlet is immersed in the mixture. Leave for about two hours, then repeat if necessary.

WINDOWS

Treat **general stains** with a mild solution of vinegar or ammonia, or try cold tea. **Paint marks** should be tackled immediately: scrape off the excess, then treat with white spirit or nail varnish remover. If the paint has hardened, soften it first with white spirit. **Putty stains** can be softened with white spirit, then scraped off. **Bad stains** can be removed by spraying the area with proprietary oven cleaner. Allow to dry, wipe off.

WOOD FURNITURE

Furniture with a veneered or French polished finish needs very special care when treating stains. In the case of antique furniture, always get a professional's opinion first.

Spirit stains (including alcohol, perfume and some medicines) should be treated immediately as they can dissolve surface finishes, especially French polish. Blot, then wipe up immediately what you have spilled with cold water rubbing the wood with the palm of your hand as it dries. French-polished furniture will almost certainly need professional treatment to restore its shine. If the stain persists

187

on other surfaces and is still fresh, try rubbing with a paste of oil and cigarette ash worked in with a circular motion. Waxed surfaces will need re-doing after this treatment.

Blood stains should be mopped up, sprinkled with salt and then wiped over. If the wood has been affected, rub gently with fine sandpaper and rub down with a hydrogen peroxide solution. Use 1 part of peroxide to 6 parts of water. Do not use this treatment on French-polished furniture as it will damage the finish.

Dents in solid wood can sometimes be treated by filling the hollow with very hot water and letting it soak in, so that the fibres swell.

Heat marks which usually appear as white rings, can be tackled by rubbing turpentine into them, going in the direction of the grain, not round in circles.

Water marks should be treated in the same way as heat marks. If this fails, then try rubbing metal polish into the marks, going in the direction of the grain. Water marks in solid wood can be treated by rubbing with very fine steel wool dipped in liquid wax floor or furniture polish.

Ink stains need quick treatment: blot, dab with bleach and blot again. Do not rub or you may be left with a bleached spot. Rinse well afterwards. Old stains can be tackled with a proprietary wood bleach.

Scratches can sometimes be saved in solid wood furniture if you pour hot water over the affected area to make the wood swell. If this fails, disguise by rubbing with a wax crayon of a similar shade to the wood or shoe polish, eyeliner or a proprietary scratch dressing.

Cigarette burns and scorch marks: if the mark is a light one, rub with metal polish, going with the grain of the wood. If the wood has a wax finish, rub with turpentine instead. If the surface is roughened and blackened, scrape with a sharp craft knife, and then rub with very fine sand paper. If necessary fill with wood stopping, then tint to match the table with the right shade of shoe or professional wood polish.

Finger marks: rub with a soft cloth dampened with a solution of 1 part vinegar to 8 parts water. Rinse, dry well afterwards.

WOOD, PAINTED

General stains should come off in a hot, mild solution of washing soda or strong solution of washing-up liquid. Do not use abrasives on gloss painted surfaces or they will rub off the shine. To clean off stains before repainting, use a strong solution of sugar soap.

"Don't Spoil the Ship For a Ha'p'orth of Tar"

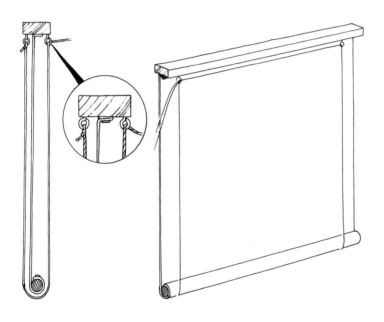

Tips on machine care, furniture care and improvizing

Machine
and furniture care

MACHINE FAULTS

Who to telephone: If your machine develops a fault, it pays to telephone the manufacturer, rather than the shop you bought it from, unless the latter has a Service Department. When you obtain the machine, write out the address and telephone number you need on a sticky label and glue in place somewhere handy on the machine.

Appliance documents: If for any reason you have to return an electrical appliance to the manufacturer for repair under guarantee, you will need the receipt or guarantee registration card that came with it. The best thing is to keep all documents relating to electrical appliances, including instruction books and serial numbers, in a safe place.

Plugs: Always pull the plug out of the wall socket before examining any electrical machine for faults.

Sockets: Before you unscrew the plug on an appliance that has stopped working, plug it into another socket which houses something you know is working. It could be that a power cut, or a faulty socket, is an explanation for the failure, not the machine.

MACHINE MAINTENANCE

Flexes: Keep flexes of portable household items like irons, hairdryers, kettles, as short as possible, whilst still allowing room for manoeuvre. You are then less likely to trip over them or hook them up in something.

Short flexes: If the flex on a household appliance is too short to reach the socket, always plug into an extension lead rather than join an extra length of flex on to the existing one. For a more permanent arrangement, the entire flex should be replaced by a professional.

Filter cleaning: Save on unnecessary visits from the repair man. Clean the filters of washing machines, tumbler driers and dishwashers, whether they seem to need it or not. This will help to keep the machines running smoothly.

Surgical tape: Use wide surgical tape to make temporary repairs on household hoses until you are able to replace them.

Frayed flexes: Generally speaking, it is dangerous to repair frayed flexes, even with insulating tape, although this will work as an emergency measure. It is much safer to replace them instead.

Hoses: Make sure that the hoses on your washing machine or dishwasher are free from kinks, are not pinched against another appliance or against the wall. Otherwise the machine may not fill or empty properly.

Blocked hoses: Check the outlet hose on washers and dishwashers from time to time, it can become blocked, with the result that the contents of the machine will stay sodden. Most outlet hoses are attached to the machine by means of a clip and can be easily removed. You can then check for blockages by looking through them or running a wire up them.

Door seals: Clean regularly round the door seals of dishwashers, washing machines to make sure that they stay watertight.

Dishwashers: Never put real silverware in contact with other metal items in a dishwasher. Otherwise it may become marked and pitted.

193

Spin drier: Always make sure that the load in your spin drier is evenly distributed, otherwise it could cause bumping, excessive vibration and possibly damage the machine. Also, the clothes will not be dried efficiently.

Tumbler drier: Never fill a tumbler drier more than two-thirds full of clothes. Make sure that they have been well wrung out or spin-dried first to save money.

REFRIGERATORS AND FREEZERS

Position: To save money when running a refrigerator or a freezer, site it in the coolest possible place, leave it at least an inch from the wall to allow the air to circulate and hot air to escape.

Door seal check: Check for a faulty door seal on refrigerators and freezers by putting a sheet of writing paper over the door edge, then shutting the door. If it is difficult to pull out, the seal is intact. If it comes away easily, the seal needs replacing.

Noisy refrigerator: If your refrigerator or freezer is making a great deal of noise, it is probably not standing on a level surface. Adjust the leg screws accordingly or level it up by placing a sliver of wood under one leg.

Dusting: Dust the unit at the back of your refrigerator regularly. A build-up of dust and dirt can cause the motor to run excessively.

When not in use: If you are not going to use the refrigerator for any length of time, always defrost and clean it first. Always leave the door propped open – otherwise mildew will form and an unpleasant smell will develop inside.

Ice-cube trays: Put a sheet of waxed paper under your ice-cube trays before you put them in the freezing compartment of the refrigerator. It stops the tray from sticking to the bottom.

Shelf use: When filling the refrigerator, store raw meat and fish in the coldest zone, cooked food and fats in the centre and salad items in the base. Dairy products and eggs should be stored in the door.

Wrapping: All food should be wrapped in the refrigerator to stop it from drying out. Strong smelling foods should be wrapped with cling-film to stop odours escaping and contaminating other food.

Warm food: Never put warm food in the refrigerator, it will cause it to ice up more quickly.

Broken racks: Broken pieces of plastic rack or accidental holes in the plastic in a refrigerator can sometimes be repaired with a resin repair kit sold in car accessory shops. Always allow it to dry thoroughly before re-using the refrigerator.

VACUUM CLEANERS

Blocked hose: If a vacuum cleaner hose becomes blocked, try reversing it by putting the nozzle on to the suction end, in the hope that will shift the blockage.

Spares: Always keep a spare rubber ring or fan belt to hand for your vacuum cleaner. They have a habit of breaking at times when the shop is shut.

ELECTRICAL GOODS

Steam iron: Always use distilled water when filling a steam iron or it will fur up in time and become faulty.

Kettle: Never fill your electric kettle when it is still plugged into the socket, and always make sure that the element is covered.

Toaster: Save on chores by standing your electric toaster on a tray to catch the crumbs. Remember to clean out the toaster's own crumb compartment regularly. Always switch off and unplug the appliance first.

Electric blankets: Remember to get your electric blanket serviced during the summer months.

GAS APPLIANCES

Ventilation: If you are using gas appliances in a room, remember that there must be adequate ventilation or they will not work properly. In particular, never block up air bricks or built-in ventilators.

Water heaters: Do not run small 'instantaneous' gas water heaters for more than five minutes at a time. Otherwise you may burn out the appliance.

COOKERS AND HEATING

Ovens: Always take a look inside the oven before you turn it on. You may have inadvertently left a dish or a baking tin with food in it, inside.

Radiant fires: Always keep the reflectors of radiant fires shining and clean to get the maximum benefit from them. Use metal polish and a soft duster to bring up the shine.

Radiators: Patchy heat on radiators is almost certainly caused by an air block. Keep a special venting key to hand to turn the valve and let the air out. Always place a bowl underneath the valve when you are doing so as a little dirty water may escape, too.

Wood-burning stoves: If you are using a wood-burning stove, or burning wood in a fireplace, remember that the chimney will need sweeping more frequently than if you are burning coal. Usual chimney sweeping intervals are: wood, 3 times a year; coal, twice a year. If you are burning smokeless fuel, then the chimney will only need attention once a year.

FURNITURE

Leg marks: To stop the legs of furniture marking the floor, glue small pieces of foam plastic to their bases.

Wall marks: To avoid the backs of sofas and armchairs from hitting and marking the wall, fix thick strips of draught excluder to them.

Upholstery studs: If you are putting decorative upholstery studs or tacks into a piece of furniture, fix a tape measure alongside the seam with masking tape. It will then give you regular marked intervals to guide you.

Protective covers: To protect the arms and backs of newly upholstered furniture, ask the store to supply you with an extra length of material. Use this to make protecting covers. The fabric can also be sprayed with silicone water and dirt repellant before use.

Screws: When screwing small items like knobs on drawers or doors in place, dip the screws into a little nail varnish before you use them. They go in more easily, set hard and won't rust.

Plastic foam: If you are stuffing a cushion with pieces of plastic foam, rub some fabric softener over the palms of your hands first. This will stop the foam from sticking to them.

CHAIRS

Cane seats: If the cane seat of a chair has become stretched and is sagging, try this method of tightening it up: sponge it carefully on both upper and lower sides with hot soapy water. Then leave it to dry, away from heat, preferably in the open air. It should shrink back to its original shape.

Wobbles: A table or chair that wobbles may have loose joints. If these are screwed in place, replace the existing screw with a larger one, or put a plastic plug into the hole and re-screw.

TABLE TOPS

Working tables: To avoid unnecessary scratches when using a dining table as a work table – i.e. for anything from sewing machines to typewriters – have a special heavy duty cloth to hand cut from thick plastic. Don't be tempted to use sheets of newspaper, etc., because they may shift during working without your noticing it.

Scratches: To avoid items like book-ends, candlesticks, lamp bases from scratching the polished top of a table, cut out pieces of felt or wool from a discarded jacket to fit them and glue to the base. Or, use foam plastic held in place with a suitable adhesive.

Large tablemats: Patchwork squares made from crocheted odds and ends of string make good tablemats to take large dishes.

FURNISHINGS AND ACCESSORIES

Newspaper: Use thick layers of newspaper as underfelt for a carpet. It not only saves wear but keeps in heat and cuts down noise.

Curtain lining: When lining curtains, leave the bottom hem of the lining unstitched. Hang the curtains for a week to allow the fabric to stretch and any creases to drop out, then hand-hem the lining in situ.

Net curtains: Hang unpatterned net curtains upside down from time to time, they will last much longer.

Waste paper baskets: Large party beer tins, covered with the type of adhesive plastic sheeting used for shelving, make good waste paper baskets.

Sheets: Give plain sheets a luxury look by sewing a band of broderie anglaise, gingham or lace, along the top turn down. Add a matching edge of frill to pillows.

Bathmats: Several same-sized bath towels that have become worn, can be quilted together to make a useful bath or beach mat. Sew decorative patches over the worn places.

Oil cloths: Old-fashioned oil cloths can be given a new lease of life if you rub the surface over with beaten white of egg, using a soft cloth. When it has dried it can be polished with a duster to make it shine.

Odd pieces of soap: Another way with odd pieces of soap: Put them into a basin with a few drops of glycerine, steam in a pan of boiling water until the mixture is soft. Allow to almost cool, press it into shape of a tablet (see also page 64).

Decorative cord: Use nail varnish or sticky tape to stop decorative cord unravelling until you have time to tackle it.

Fuzzy fabric: 'Shave' the surface of a fabric with a razor blade to remove small balls of fuzz, or, rub with very fine sandpaper.

Gift tags: Save last year's Christmas cards to make gift tags for the following year: cut out colourful decorations, thread with a cotton tie, write a message on the back.

NYLON TIGHTS AND STOCKINGS

Vacuuming: Fasten a piece of nylon tights over the nozzle of a vacuum cleaner. You can then use it to vacuum out the insides of drawers and other difficult places, without blowing the contents around. It's also a useful way to pick up contact lenses out of carpets.

Storage: Use discarded nylon stockings to store onions and other items. Hang them up in a corner or a cupboard. They'll store better that way.

Fastenings: Old nylon stockings make good ties to fasten the tops of large plastic garbage bags.

Odd stockings: If you have a lot of odd stockings, boil them up quickly together in a large saucepan, leave them to cool and they should all come out the same colour. Add a teabag or two if you want to intensify the shade.

Starching: If you apply a little starch to tights when you wash them, they are much less likely to snag and are easier to put on.

NEW LEASE OF LIFE

Bras: Turn a white bra into a flesh-coloured one on a temporary basis – to wear under see-through clothes for instance. Soak it in a solution of 60 ml (4 tablespoons) of instant coffee to 1 litre (2 pints) of water. Check the colour after a while, rinse in cold water and dry. After a few washes, the colour will come out.

Fabric shoes: Linen and canvas running shoes and sandals will resist dirt much longer if you spray them with fabric protector before you wear them. Spray white tennis shoes with starch for the same reason.

Make-up bags: A thick polythene bag makes a good plastic liner for a decorative fabric make-up bag.

REPAIRING AND MENDING

Torn pages: The torn page of a book can be glued back together again with the white of an egg. Place the pieces in position on a smear of egg white, cover lightly on top with egg white and allow to dry thoroughly before you move.

Broken china: When mending china, clean the breaks first with cottonwool dipped in neat hydrogen peroxide, to remove any discoloration.

Broken crockery: A cup, plate or saucer that has just one break in it can be mended with an epoxy resin glue – colour it to match the china with powdered artists colours.

Waxing a leak: Paraffin wax can be used to mend a leaking vase, just coat the inside with a thick layer and allow to dry.

Filling a crack: A hairline crack in crockery that is causing a leak can be sealed by simmering the offending article in milk for about an hour. The milk should fill the crack and coagulate inside it making a seal.

Black dye: When dyeing a piece of fabric black, it's a good idea to use an equal quantity of blue dye. This avoids that green tell tale tinge that many home-coloured black garments have.

Cracked ivory: Restore the look of cracked ivory or bone pieces by dipping them in white melted candle wax. Wipe off any excess and leave them to set. Provided you keep them away from direct heat, the cracks should not show.

Holed umbrella: Use iron-on mending tape to repair a hole in an umbrella. Place the tape on the underside of the cover then press on top with a warm iron.

Clothes' patches: If you are patching clothes, use pinking shears to cut out the pieces of material to save having to turn under the edges.

Improvization

INSIDE AND OUTSIDE THE HOUSE

Carpet off-cuts: You can carpet a room very cheaply – or even for free. Carpet shops sell off cheaply, or sometimes give away, sample pieces of carpet (sometimes quite large) when they change lines. Ring up carpet shops in your area and ask. the pieces can be glued or stitched together to make a large patchwork carpet.

Patterned flooring: If you can't afford carpets for a room, you can improve the look of the floor by stencilling it. Buy ready-made stencils or cut your own from stencil paper. Hold them in place with masking tape and use either spray paint or use ordinary gloss paint with a stencil brush. A final coat of polyurethane varnish will also give a longer lasting finish.

From door to work surface: An old door makes a handy work surface. If you use the hinges to attach it to the wall and fit hinged legs, you can fold it away when not in use.

Build your own barbecue: Use a few bricks and two wire grills for a cheap home barbecue set. Make it half a metre (two feet) square and two bricks high. Remove one brick to allow air to circulate. Put one of the wire grills on top of the bricks – this is for the charcoal. Build up the square to waist height, then put the other grill on top for the food.

Free-standing shelves: Make your own bookcase quickly and easily. Simply stack planks or floorboards on top of bricks, which act as spacers. Don't build more than four planks high, or the structure will become unsteady.

Home-made blind: An old broomstick can be made into the basis of a cheap rolled blind. First cut it to the width of the window. Choose a piece of material and cut this to the width and length of the window allowing for, then making, narrow hems. Tack one end to a batten (25 × 50 mm/2 × 1 inches) the width of the window and the other to the broomstick. Fix two long pieces of string to the batten a short way in from the edges of, and behind, the material. Fix two screw eyes opposite the string in front of the material. Roll the material up around the broomstick to the top of the window. Pass the two pieces of string through the two screw eyes. Use the string to raise and lower the blind.

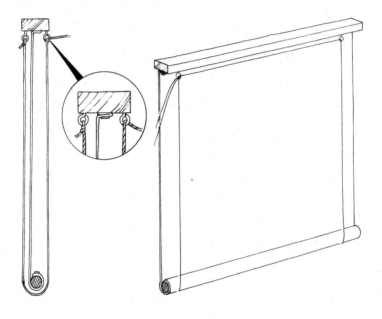

Hang it all: Paint a length of old garden trellis a bright colour, attach it to the kitchen wall, hang a few butcher's hooks from it and you will have instant extra storage for untidy kitchen utensils.

Medicine containers: Four litre (two pint) icecream containers are ideal for keeping first aid and medical supplies in. Remember to keep medicine out of reach of children.

Screw-top jars: Save screw top jars to make under-shelf storage for odds and ends. Simply screw the jar lid to the bottom of a wooden shelf – use at least two screws. Now the jar will hang under the shelf and can be removed with just a twist, leaving the lid still in place.

Improvized wardrobe: Use narrow alcoves for hanging clothes. Attach two or three lengths of strong chain to the wall at different heights near the top. Use fairly large linked chain, so that the coat hangers will slot into them. Attach one end to the wall and let it hang vertically. Use this to hang clothes from, so that they overlap. Hang a piece of curtain over the front of the alcove if you wish.

Kitchen knife holder: Save empty cotton reels to make into a useful kitchen knife holder. Nail a row of them shoulder-to-shoulder on to a piece of board. Add another row 75–100 mm (3 to 4 in) below the first row, taking care to line the two rows up. Attach the board to the kitchen wall and slip the knives in between the reels, so that they hang by their handles.

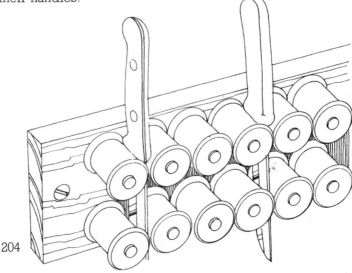

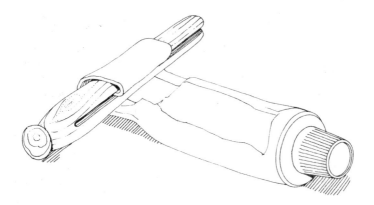

A tight squeeze: Use an old-fashioned clothes peg as a 'key' to get the most out of toothpaste tubes. Slip the peg over the end of the tube when about half of the paste has been used. Twist the tube around the peg to get all the paste out.

Plunger to the rescue: If you accidentally pull one of the handles off a chest of drawers, you may find the drawer impossible to pull out. Wet the end of a rubber plunger and use this as a giant sucker to pull the drawer out.

Handy tool holder: Cut the finger ends off an old leather glove, cut two slots in the palm and thread on a belt for a useful tool holster.

Cork cushions: An old cork will help to save your fingers, when you are rummaging in your odds and ends drawer. Use the cork as a pin cushion for nails, drawing pins and other sharp objects.

There's life in an old paintbrush: A matted old paintbrush can still be of use – cut off the matted bristles to leave a handy dusting down brush to use before decorating.

Plant markers: Save the children's iced lolly sticks to use as plant markers – just write on them with a permanent marker. You can cut one end to a point with a sharp knife to make it easier to stick in the soil.

Bottle top bird scarer: If you grow your own fruit or vegetables, make a useful bird-scarer this way. Save foil milk bottle tops, when you have about thirty, thread them loosely on to a piece of strong cotton or string, with a knot between to make sure they are separated. Hang up between two pieces of bamboo a little way above the ground. The noise and the flashing produced as they move in the wind is enough to keep most birds away.

Non-rust cans: Aluminium drink cans make good paint-brush holders – they won't rust and discolour the paint. Use a knife to cut off the top of the can, then trim any rough edges with scissors. If there are still jagged pieces, either file them with coarse sandpaper or fold over the edges to the inside of the can. Wash carefully before using.

Screen it: Screens are convenient to add privacy to bedsits. To make your own, hinge together four louvred doors or shutters with attractive brass hinges.

Measuring pinta: If you need to measure a pint of liquid but do not have a measuring jug, use a clean milk bottle instead. You could make similar use of a litre wine bottle, if measuring in metric.

RECYCLING IDEAS

Bright plant pots: Cans that have contained tinned food make good containers for small plants – clean them thoroughly, then paint them in bright colours and they will look completely different. Empty paint tins also make cheap and cheerful holders for outdoor plant pots, once they have been cleaned and painted.

Freezer fillers: Fill empty plastic lemonade or squash

bottles with water and use them to fill space in your freezer, if it is low on food. A full freezer functions more efficiently.

Egg-box starter kits: Egg-boxes can be used as starter kits for seeds – fill the hollows with soil or vermiculite, sow the seed in them. They're useful for starting off seed potatoes too, as they hold them in the correct position.

"Strike While the Iron Is Hot"

All about
washing, drying and ironing

Washing wisdom

GOOD PRACTICE

Bicarbonate of soda: One of those magic substances that can work all kinds of wonders, from improving your baking to cleaning the oven quickly, so it's hardly surprising that it can help with the weekly wash, too. If you substitute a tablespoon of soda bicarbonate for a quarter of a cup of your normal washing powder it will not only save you the cost of that powder, but it will also help to free the grime from the fibres as well as acting as a water softener. Rinse thoroughly.

Bulky articles: Wet bulky articles before putting them in the washing machine, to make fitting them in easier but be careful not to overload your machine (follow the instruction booklet to find out about maximum loading). Bear in mind that a full load is harder to rinse.

Empty pockets: Check pockets of any garment before you put it into the washing machine. Soggy bank notes which go through the whole washing cycle won't buy the groceries; paper clips, coins or pen tops can wreak their own particular kind of havoc with the wash!

Garment labels: Don't take a guess at the programme for any fabric. Instead, take a few minutes to go through the clothes to be washed, looking at each label and sorting them into little heaps according to the instructions.

Economy load: Remember (if your machine has one) that you can always use the economy half load programme on your washing machine for a small wash.

Mix garments: If, of course, you find you only have a few things to be washed on one programme and you don't want to waste time, money and electricity, then you can mix garments requiring a quite different wash treatment, but in this case you must wash *all* of them on the programme given for the most *delicate fabrics* and do not mix dark and light colours.

Delicate fibres: Some garment labels giving the fabric content are as long as a laundry list as there are so many different fibres in the one material. For practical purposes and to be safe, pick out the most delicate of the fibres in the mix and wash according to the instructions on its care label.

Loading: Load your machine properly following the machine manufacturer's instructions, if you want to get clothes washed well. Some wash programmes should only have small loads, so check the instructions for your machine carefully. Always remember that it's better to do two washes than stuff a few extra things in; big loads rarely give the best wash.

Low lather powders: Though designed for automatic machines these can be used for other machines too. A good reason for using them is that you end up with much less scum in the water than with the powders intended for non-automatics.

Ordinary washing powder: Don't use ordinary powder in a front-loading automatic or a top loader with a revolving drum if you want to keep your clothes in good shape. The drum action causes too much froth with an ordinary powder, which in turn causes fabrics to get squeezed hard against the side of the drum and prevents them from getting a proper wash.

Hand wash: When you're washing garments by hand it's absolutely essential to make sure that the powder is properly dissolved before you put the garments into the water. If you don't, you'll get nasty little white bits sticking to the clothes when they're dry. If you're using warm water for the wash, put the required amount of powder into a container, pour boiling water on to it, stir until thoroughly dissolved, then add the solution to the warm water in the bowl or sink.

Soaking: Soaking heavily soiled clothes before you put them through the regular washing programme will usually result in cleaner clothes. However, *always* check the garment label first. Don't be too impatient, a long soak gives the powder time to get to work and flush out the worst grime and stains. So organize yourself and your clothes the night before washday and soak white things overnight and coloured articles for at least two hours. Start the soak with hand hot, never boiling, water.

Special finishes: Never soak garments made of silk, wool, leather or any fabrics which are not colourfast and be wary of any fabric with a special finish (such as waterproof or flame-resistant clothing).

Trimmings: Any garments with metal trimmings. buckles, heavy zips, metal buttons and so on don't take to soaking too well either, so if you can't remove the trimmings, don't soak.

Soap: Soap is splendid stuff and is essential to keep many of our clothes clean, but too much of it can definitely have a dulling effect on clothes. Black garments end up with a 'bloom' on them and white things can either go grey or yellowish. One way to make sure you get all the soap out of them is to add 1 tablespoon of vinegar to the rinsing water.

Suds: If you see that during the last rinse on the washing machine cycle there still seem to be suds left in the water, or the clothes feel ever so slightly 'slimy' when you take them out, try the vinegar treatment here, too. Pop the things back in again for one more rinse and add a teacupful of vinegar.

Test for colour fastness: Dip a small section of the garment into a solution of washing powder mixed in warm water, then place the material between two sheets of blotting paper on your ironing board and press with a warm iron. If the colour goes on to the paper or the shade of the garment changes appreciably through the application of heat (if it goes dark, for instance, then goes back to the same shade as the rest of the fabric), then wash the item separately.

Rescue plan: If you've forgotten to test garments for colour fastness, or your husband has slipped a pair of bright new socks into the washing machine when your back was turned, and you get colour transferring on to other garments, the best chance of getting rid of it or lessening the impact is to take prompt action. Should you be lucky enough to spot what's happened as the clothes dance past the glass door of the machine then switch off straight away. Turn the dial to allow the water to drain away, switch on and, when drained, switch off again. Take out all the clothes. Separate those affected by the colour and put these back into the machine again, add powder and select a wash programme as hot as the fabrics will take and let everything go right through the wash cycle again. With a bit of luck and some help from the washing powder and the water, the colours will fade considerably, perhaps disappear altogether.

TYPES OF CLOTHING

Jeans: Blue jeans all fade in the wash to a greater or lesser degree. However, if they begin to fade in streaks and lines it's not the fabric that's at fault but the way you're washing them. To avoid the streaks, turn inside out before washing.

Bras: Bras take a lot of punishment from perspiration which can rot elastic. Wash them every day if at all possible or at least every other day. They should dry overnight. If hand washing, do not rub, twist or wring. Rinse two or three times in clear warm water. Gently ease into shape and hang to dry away from heat. Padded bras need special treatment if they, and you, are to keep in shape. If they have an interlining of foam rubber, a washing machine can damage it. Wash in hand hot water, rinse thoroughly and dry well away from heat.

Protective garments: Dungarees, overalls and other such garments worn in the garden or the workshop can be difficult to launder. Dip the garments in a fairly thin starch after you have washed them, then allow them to drip dry in the garden: washing will be much easier the next time round.

Girdles: Like bras, girdles have a longer life if they are washed every day. Latex and nylon should need only a quick dip, a quick spin and then be left to dry overnight.

Embroidered items: Hand-embroidered blouses and scarves often come from third world countries, and such garments sometimes do not have labels giving wash instructions, while those which do are not always as clear as they might be, so it's always wise to take a few precautions. Before you wash any embroidered item put it into a solution of salt and water (1 tablespoon of salt to 1 litre (2 pints) of water). This will sometimes help set the colour and prevent any tendency to run. Leave in the solution for a couple of hours, then rinse out the salt with lots of cold water before washing very carefully in cool to warm water. It is best to wash by hand, unless the care label recommends otherwise. A touch of vinegar in the final rinsing water (a tablespoon to a bowl of water) will help revive the colours and bring them back to freshness.

Leisure wear: Jogging and leisure wear (and even some of those chunky sweaters) made from synthetics have 'Hand wash only' tags on them. If you don't discover this until you take your purchase out of the carrier bag at home, then don't despair, hand washing needn't be all that much of a chore! The quickest and most efficient way to get the dirt out of even the grubbiest garment is to use the same powder as you do for your automatic – this makes the grime literally flow out before your very eyes. For one sweater add something less than 1 tablespoon of powder to a basin full of water. Give the garment a gentle squeeze, pop it into your washing machine and programme it to a cool rinse and a short spin. When the label on the garment says 'Don't machine wash' the 'Don't' doesn't include rinsing and spinning, it's quite safe to do it.

214

Coloured socks: Leg warmers and chunky socks usually come in bright and cheerful colours, but be wary about washing them along with other items of clothing unless you're quite certain they're colourfast. While many garments, cord jeans for instance, do make it clear on the label that they need to be washed separately, socks rarely seem to provide such information.

Silk blouses: Silk blouses are extremely luxurious to wear but can be laborious to wash. Wash them by hand using warm soapy water, then lots of cool to rinse.

Swimsuits: Swimwear suffers from salt in sea water and chemicals in pool water. If you're putting a swimsuit away for the winter give it a good soaking in cold water to take out the salt, then wash and dry. If, on the other hand, you haven't got further than the local swimming pool, the suit could be affected by chemicals in the water, so soak it in $2\frac{1}{4}$ litres (half a gallon) of water, to which you've added 2 teaspoons of borax, before washing in the usual way. Always rinse swimsuits in fresh water after every wear.

Tights: Tights tend to get snagged in the washing process if you do not take precautions. It can happen all too easily if they go into the washing machine along with a jumble of other items with zips and hooks and sometimes the drum itself can develop a slight roughness which is equally hazardous. Pop the tights into something like a pillowcase for protection before putting them into the washing machine. An alternative 'tights protector' is a square scarf. Knot it securely round the tights to form a pouch similar to Dick Whittington's.

Synthetics: Synthetic materials are unfortunately not always as easy to care for as one might imagine. Washing them the wrong way, for instance, can lead to nylon blouses acquiring a permanently crushed look, body-hugging ribbed polo neck sweaters can very easily turn into loose baggy garments if you wash them at too high a temperature. To retain that spring and cling, wash at a lowish temperature, and keep handling down to a minimum.

215

Drying

Dresses: Washable dresses can be dried on hangers in much the same way as they are hung in a wardrobe, but those with pleated skirts should be hung by the waistband with the pleats falling straight. Don't skimp on the pegs – use them along the waist seam.

Towel treatment: Drip drying something large like a coat can be rather messy – no one wants puddles all over the floor. So if the weather won't allow the garment to be hung outside, try the towel treatment. Absorb excess moisture, or as much as possible, by rolling the coat in a towel before hanging up.

Radiators: Things like socks and leg warmers will dry much more quickly if you hang them on a clothes' drier near a radiator. Shirts and blouses can be put on a hanger and then hung on the clothes' drier. This minimizes the need for ironing as most of the creases will drop out.

Running colours: Sometimes running colours are a problem even at the drying stage. Hang striped garments, which have a tendency to run, with the stripes running down vertically. The quicker such garments are dried, the less chance there is of dye running. You can spin dry after washing in coolish water, then shake the garment out immediately.

After starching: Starched clothes should not be left out on the washing line after they've dried if there's a sharp wind about. The wind can have the effect of blowing out all the newly acquired crispness from collars and cuffs and leaving them quite limp.

Damp pockets: Trousers often seem perfectly dry until you feel the pockets, which are still soggy. Avoid this by turning the trousers inside out before pegging them out on the line. The pockets will flap about in the breeze and will keep pace with the rate at which the rest of the fabric is drying. Open zips too (which you will have taken care to close during the washing process, of course, to avoid damage) then the air will be able to circulate all round the double thickness of material at these points.

Tumble driers: Don't overload the machine and don't put your socks and underwear in with large items like sheets if you want to get good results. Dripping wet clothes should never be put straight into a tumble drier; spin them first following the instructions on the care label. Taking out the garments just as soon as the cooling period finishes also helps to prevent any creases setting into the fabric. Try not to mix several types of fabrics in the one load as each may require different heat settings and drying times to get the best results. Dry for the shortest possible time, as overdrying can harm fabric.

White wool: White wool garments must be dried well away from the noonday sun. Sunlight has a tendency to turn such garments yellowish. Other forms of direct heating inside can have a similar effect. Sunlight can also fade coloured fabrics so always take care when drying in very sunny weather.

Nylon pile: Coats and jackets made of nylon pile fabric should be shaken several times as they're drying on the line. This will help restore the fluffy look to the pile.

Extra space: Spread a net or nylon mesh over the bath, fixed in four corners by suction cups, this will give you extra drying room.

Clothes rack: A length of ladder that is too old to be trusted to support your weight can make a useful clothes rack. Hang it from the bathroom or kitchen ceiling from four hooks fastened into the joists.

217

Ironing

Checklist of points for making ironing easier:
Check that the item is at the right degree of dampness for ironing.
Fill a steam iron and select the steam indicator before switching on the iron. If not using steam, then dampen very dry items and roll up.
Make sure the iron and the board are clean before you start.
Always start ironing on a part of the garment hidden in wear, just to be on the safe side.
If you can sit down and be comfortable, then do.
Put your basket of clothes on one side of the board and have a clothes drying rack on the other – small items can be draped over the rack, things like blouses can be hung on with hangers. To take longer things like dresses you can screw a piece of wood on to the back of the kitchen or cupboard door near where you do your ironing – put a few cup hooks into the wood, then simply hang the ironed dresses on hangers on to the hook.
A top cover of silver milium fabric over your board can make ironing easier. It reflects the heat, retains the damp. Always iron in the direction of the selvedge.
Iron a garment methodically – going from one section to the next in sequence – don't dash about all over the place with the iron.
Iron double parts first on thick materials and last on thin materials.
Iron with smooth, slow strokes – back and forwards at the same pace.

Clean hems: Clean the floor underneath the ironing board.

Sheets and long dresses drag on the floor as you iron them and can pick up dust in the process. If you put an old sheet or blanket down on the floor and stand the ironing board on top of this, hems of garments shouldn't get marks on them.

Crisp creases: For a crease you could cut butter with, turn trouser legs inside out and rub some hard yellow soap down the inside of the crease, then turn right side out and press with a damp cloth. Don't soak the pressing cloth or you'll run the risk of the soap forming suds.

Damp cloth: A damp cloth is your greatest ally when it comes to ironing materials like corduroy and crêpe. Turn the garments inside out and iron with a damp cloth using gentle pressure. If you are dealing with a double thickness of material, trouser legs perhaps, then try this: fold a towel to approximately the same width as the leg and slip it inside before ironing; this will save the pile being damaged as it rubs against the other side of the leg. To obtain the crease in the trouser leg, turn the right way round again, put a folded towel underneath and a damp cloth on top and press very lightly.

Ironing blouses and shirts: Tackle those areas where there's a double thickness of material first at collar and cuffs, pressing first on the wrong side, then on the right. Iron sleeves next, then work your way round from the right side via the centre and finish with the left front. If, of course, you happen to be left-handed, then you'll want to start with the left front and work round that way.

Freshly ironed garments: Anything which is still warm and sometimes ever so slightly damp as well, will crease twice as easily as when it's completely cool, so don't wear garments immediately.

Hangers: Do put blouses, jackets, trousers and dresses on to a hanger the moment they are off the ironing board . . . if you drape them over a chair they'll develop creases at an amazing rate and without any help from you!

Go with the grain: Always move in the direction of the grain of the fabric and use long smooth strokes, with the following exceptions: very fine wool should be ironed with a light circular motion; viscose should be ironed diagonally.

Perfect finish: Garments which are too wet will have a poor finish, those which are too dry won't come up smooth and crisp. But as with every rule, there's always an exception! Shantung, tussore, chiffon, georgette and crêpe should be quite dry before they're ironed.

Seams: On delicate garments seams can become unsightly and obvious if ironed the wrong way so that the extra material used in the seam shows through the surface as a hard ridge. There's no denying that it takes time and care to avoid the seam showing on the right side, but if you want your clothes to look as though they are treated with care, it's well worth making the effort. Make up some long narrow strips of brown paper (save the paper from parcels or even from grocery bags) and keep them in a drawer near where you usually do your ironing. Push a strip under the seam allowance before you iron and no impression will show through.

Don't despair: Sometimes after you've washed a garment you get a seam puckering badly. If this happens don't despair, you can take out the kinks with a strong right arm and the iron! This should last for the first few hours of wear. Lay the seam on the board, give a firm tug to the hem, or the bottom of the leg if it's trousers, and while you are pulling the seam straight with one hand, iron with the other using a fair amount of pressure and a good head of steam.

Sorting: Sort all the garments to be ironed into different fabrics; iron those which need a cool iron first.

Soiled clothes: Dirty clothes should never be 'freshened up' by ironing. They may look a little better but the long term results can be disastrous as you could simply have set stubborn stains hard into the fabric with the heat.

Starched collars and cuffs: Starched items should be kept until last, because the starch can cling to the base of the iron and can all too easily be transferred onto the next garment as an unsightly brown mark. Clean the base of the iron immediately you have finished ironing a starched item. A quick rub over with the rough side of a damp foam washing-up pad (the sort designed for non-stick pans) should do the trick.

Steam: A satisfying hissing rising up from the fabric tells you that the iron's doing its work effectively (dry fabrics rarely iron up crisp and crease-free). There are various ways of keeping clothes damp; pick the one which suits you best. Try one of those little plant sprayers, keep it by the ironing board and use it to put a fine mist of water over clothes. A cleaned flour or sugar shaker filled with water can also be used to spot the fabric with droplets of water. Alternatively, roll up the clothes before they are really dry and store them in a large plastic bag (a bin liner will do the trick). Clothes will then stay damp until you're ready to iron them. But a word of warning here: don't leave them encased in plastic for more than twenty-four hours, otherwise you'll have mildew to get out of the clothes as well as the creases!

Ties: If you press ties the chances are that the seam will show through and you'll get a line down the middle. Cut out a piece of cardboard to correspond to the shape of the tie and put it in between the two sides of the tie before pressing. If you have narrow ties, medium ties and wide ties, then it's not a bad idea to cut out a cardboard shape to suit each of them to have on hand when you come to do the ironing. Use a damp cloth when pressing ties.

Bachelor's trick: Trousers can be pressed under the mattress overnight using an old bachelor's trick, but be careful not to strain your back lifting the mattress. Moisten the creases with a damp cloth first.

"There's Many a Slip Twixt Cup and Lip"

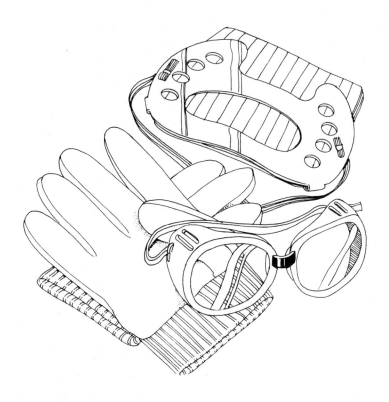

Safety hints about the house

Safety tips about the house

IN THE KITCHEN

Sharp knives: Blunt knives are even more dangerous than sharp ones because of the extra force needed to cut with them – keep yours sharp.

Loose handles: Loose saucepan handles are a danger as the handle may come off while you are carrying something hot. If the handle is screwed on, this just needs to be tightened up. If the handle is held by rivets, these can be tightened by putting one end of the rivet in contact with something hard (a brick, for example) and hitting the other end with a hammer.

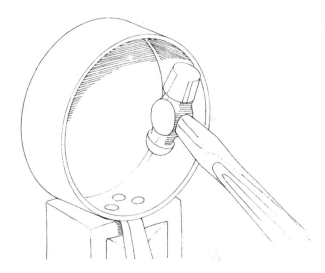

Handy surface: When planning a kitchen, try to arrange to have a surface next to the cooker on to which you can place pans from the cooker. It is dangerous to carry a heavy pan full of hot food across the kitchen.

Sensible storage: Another point to remember when planning a kitchen is that heavy items should not be stored above shoulder height. Reaching up to get a heavy pan from a top shelf is an ideal recipe for a domestic disaster. Even if the item is light, it is better to step up rather than reach up, to it. Invest in a sturdy set of steps; never balance on an old chair.

Cork it: Embed points of skewers and other sharp objects in old corks before putting them away in a drawer – that way you won't hurt your hands when you hunt for them.

Mince meat: When putting meat through a mincer use a wooden spoon, not your fingers, to push it down.

KITCHEN FIRE HAZARDS

Deep frying: When deep frying make sure the fat (without food in) doesn't come more than a third of the way up the side of the pan.

Fat on fire: If fat catches fire while you are cooking meat, sprinkle the meat and fat with bicarbonate of soda to put out the flames. When the soda is rinsed off, the meat will still be edible.

Steam: When pouring hot water out of a pan into the sink, partially fill the sink with cold water first to prevent steam from rising up and scalding your hands. Don't be put off if there seems to be more steam than usual – really hot steam is invisible, it shows up only as it cools.

Smoking oil: Remember that oil doesn't need a naked flame to light it. Once oil is sufficiently hot it will ignite on its own. Never let it get hot enough to start smoking – at this temperature, as well as being a fire hazard, it starts to break down and will make food taste bitter.

Damp heat: Never use a damp or wet teacloth for handling anything hot. The water will transmit the heat through the cloth and burn your hands.

The right clothes: When cooking, don't wear extravagant clothes that may trail and catch alight on the cooker.

Flame stopper: If a fire breaks out in the oven, don't open the oven door. Keep the door shut and turn off the heat – the fire will go out through lack of air. As an extra precaution with a gas oven, turn the mains supply off as well.

Teacloths: Never hang teacloths to dry over the cooker – this is a common cause of kitchen fires.

Safety blanket: Keep a fire blanket near the cooker to put out flames involving fat and/or electricity, then you won't be tempted to put water on the flames, which will only make matters worse.

Dry fry: Make it a rule: never put wet food into hot fat – to do so causes the fat to spit violently. Dry the food (chips, for example) with a cloth before sliding carefully into the pan.

Hot surface: Never use the surface of an electric hob as a place to leave empty pans, etc. The hob may be turned on inadvertently.

GENERAL FIRE HAZARDS

Deep ashtrays: If you smoke, use stable, deep ashtrays where there is no risk of the tray being knocked over, or the cigarette falling out of it.

Flammable products: Don't store anything flammable near the entrance to the house or under the stairs (this includes many common household products). In the event of a fire they may ignite and make it difficult for you to get out of the house.

Decorations: When buying Christmas decorations, make sure that they are flame resistant.

Low beams: After you have moved into a new house you'll find that it takes some time for you to get used to any low beams. To avoid constantly banging your head, draw attention to the doorway by hanging something brightly coloured over it. The same applies to a doorway that is frequently used by guests.

Oil heaters 1: Never attempt to fill an oil heater when it is alight, this is often the cause of a fire.

Oil heaters 2: If possible, take the heater to the source of fuel rather than vice versa, to avoid unnecessary spills inside the house.

Oil heaters 3: Never move an oil heater around the room when it is alight and do not position it in a draughty spot. Never dry clothes on it.

Smoke detectors: Most people die in fires due to asphyxiation from smoke rather than from the flames. Fit smoke detectors to give you an early warning of a fire.

T.V. grill: Make sure that the ventilation grill at the back of your television is not blocked by curtains.

Microcooking: Microwave cookers do not always heat food evenly – stir it before eating or you may be badly burned.

Rubbish fire: Cigarette ash put into a rubbish bin is a common cause of fires. Empty ashtrays into an empty tin can and pour a little water in with the ash before throwing away.

SERVICES

Mains stopcock: Make sure that everyone in the family knows where the mains water stopcock is and can turn it.

Cut-off rules: If you have coin-operated gas or electricity and it runs out, remember to turn off any appliances *before* putting more money in. Remember with gas that you will probably have to re-light pilot lights. During a power cut, the same rules apply to electrical and gas appliances.

Electricity in the bathroom: Electricity and water together are a recipe for tragedy. Never touch or operate any electrical appliances with wet hands, and never take any kind of appliance into the bathroom. The availability of electricity in the bathroom is limited deliberately to pull-cord operated light and heating fittings, and isolated shaver points, for your safety.

ELECTRICAL APPLIANCES

Cleaning: Switch off all appliances before cleaning them. The same applies when removing bread that's stuck in the toaster. Even when a toaster is switched off the elements should not be touched as they are easily damaged.

The right amp: Putting a 13 amp fuse in a plug on an appliance that draws very little current (a table light, perhaps) is almost as bad as by-passing the fuse altogether. Use a 3 amp or 5 amp fuse instead. As a guide to which to use, remember that a 3 amp fuse is for up to 600 watts and a 5 amp fuse for up to 1000 watts. Most appliances have their wattages marked on them somewhere.

Plug wiring: Keep a note of the correct way of wiring a plug in a place where you can always find it when you need it (on the inside of a tool box or the handle of a screwdriver, for example). The new colour coding for the wires is as shown below left. This replaces the previous colour coding which you will have on older appliances (below right).

NEW COLOUR CODE
GREEN/YELLOW = EARTH (E)
BROWN   = LIVE (L)
BLUE   = NEUTRAL (N)

OLD COLOUR CODE
GREEN = EARTH (E)
RED   = LIVE (L)
BLACK = NEUTRAL (N)

If the plug has a two core flex, leave the earth terminal blank.

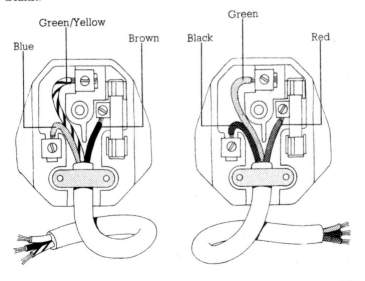

Correct wattage: Most lampshades have a maximum wattage bulb recommended by the manufacturer. Make a note of this and don't be tempted to use larger bulbs, they may cause a fire.

Cable grips: Always use the cable grips when wiring a plug. Many people 'save time' by not using them – however, if they are not used the strain on the wire will mean that the plug soon has to be rewired; it can also cause the wires to short, fusing the plug or causing a bad accident.

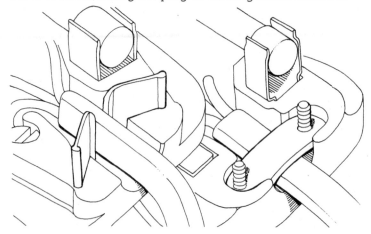

Switch off appliances: To avoid fire, unplug, or switch off at the socket, as many appliances as is possible before retiring to bed. This is particularly important for the television.

Socket adaptors: Never use more than one socket adaptor in any one socket; to do so can cause sparking and be a fire hazard.

Electrical imports: Many other countries have different, or much lower, standards when it comes to electrical safety; be watchful when buying imported items or bringing things back from holiday. If in doubt have them checked by a qualified electrician.

Fuses: Never replace the fuse in a plug with anything but the correct fuse. Never be tempted to use pieces of wire, silver foil, etc. At a pinch you can use a fuse of a lower rating if you do not have exactly the right one, but you may find it blows very easily.

Electrical check-up: If you buy a secondhand electrical appliance, have it checked by a qualified electrician before using it, even if it seems to be in perfect condition.

Extra insulation: Most tools designed for electrical work are insulated. For extra safety, if you find yourself having to use tools that are not, simply wrap insulating tape around the handles.

AND GAS APPLIANCES

Secondhand gas appliance: When considering the purchase of a secondhand gas appliance don't forget that you will need to have it checked by a qualified engineer, not only for your peace of mind, but also in order to satisfy the gas board. You should therefore add the cost of this on to the price of the item.

Gas water heater: If you have a gas water heater in the bathroom, don't get into the bath while it's running.

Back from holiday: Remember to relight any pilots on gas appliances, once you have turned on the mains supply on your return from holiday.

ELECTRIC BLANKETS

Overloaded plug: Never plug electric blankets into an adaptor which is shared with another appliance. This could cause overloading.

Avoid creases: Always make sure that an electric blanket is lying flat and smooth on the bed. Creases in it could cause the element to break.

Blanket storage: Never fold an electric blanket to store it. Instead roll it up or keep it flat on a spare bed when not in use.

Overheating: Do not leave heavy objects, such as suit cases, on a bed when the electric blanket is switched on. It could cause the wires to overheat.

HOME SECURITY

New locks: When moving into a new flat or house, it's worth changing the major locks on outside doors. If you don't do this you have no way of knowing how many keys there are in existence and who has them (anyone who had borrowed the keys from the estate agent, for example, could have had copies cut).

Prevention is best: To prevent a lock being slipped using a thin piece of plastic, knock a few carpet tacks into the frame just in front of the bolt recess. Don't knock them in all the way, just far enough for the door to close without scraping them. In this position they will block any attempt to slip the lock.

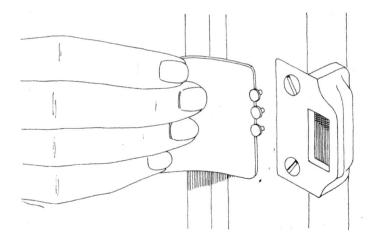

Inner doors: Don't bother to lock inside doors when going away on holiday – once a burglar has got into the house this will not stop him, it will only increase the amount of damage done.

Out of sight: Don't leave valuables on view through windows. These will only tempt people, and may give the impression that yours is a home worth burgling.

No ladders: Don't leave ladders lying around outside if you can help it. If you have to, then padlock them to something, so that they can't be moved.

Keys in the lock: Never leave keys in the lock on the inside of a door. Very often if you do a burglar can either turn it from the outside with a pair of tweezers or make a small hole in the door near the lock and turn it like that.

Mortice bolts: Where possible, fit key-operated mortice bolts rather than ordinary barrel bolts. Mortice bolts are much stronger because they are set into the door itself and from the outside the burglar has no way of knowing where and how many of them there are.

Insurance: Make sure you are fully insured. Also, keep your insurance updated in line with inflation and any new valuable contents added since the last estimate.

Beware strangers: Don't let strangers into the house without making them show you identification. Many burglars carry out thefts by tricking their way into the house.

No notes: Never leave a note on the door saying that you are out, or when you will be back.

Safe for people

WITH CHILDREN IN MIND

Drink bottles: Never use bottles that once contained soft drinks to store anything else in. Small children may well recognize the bottle and help themselves.

Stair gates: Use safety gates across all stairways until you are confident that a small child is old enough to cope with them.

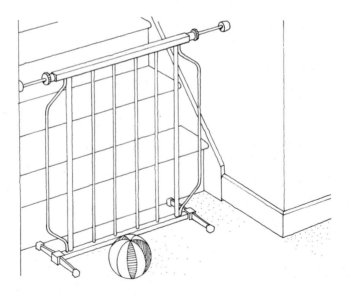

Baby bath: A baby can easily slip in a bath and bang its head. To prevent this, put a small towel or flannel on the bottom of the bath before filling.

Safe saucepans: Small children will reach up to grab at anything. When cooking keep all saucepans and frying pans turned in from the edge of the cooker. Put a guard rail round the edge, and never leave a child alone in the kitchen. If possible, use the kind of pans that have two small handles, one on each side, rather than those with just one large one.

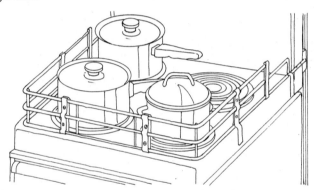

Storage places: If you have a child about your home for the first time, you will have to alter some of the places that you usually keep things – don't keep cleaners and chemicals under the sink, for example.

Eating code: Children are not always good at remembering which growing things are safe to eat and which are not. To be on the safe side tell them not to eat anything that is growing.

Washing machines: If you have small children, make sure that the door of your washing machine and tumbler drier cannot be opened while the machines are running. When buying a new machine, get one where the door can be locked when not in use.

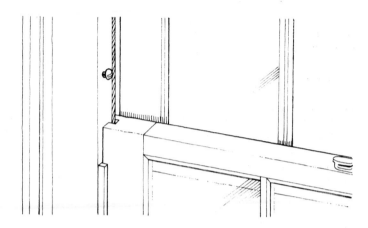

Sash windows: If you have small children around, make sure that they can't fall out of a sash window by putting a screw in the way of the runner 15 centimetres (six inches) above the top of the lower sash. You'll still be able to open the window for fresh air, but not far enough to be a danger to children.

Socket covers: Although modern sockets incorporate a mechanism to prevent children pushing things into them, accidents can happen. Be on the safe side, use plastic socket covers when the socket is not in use.

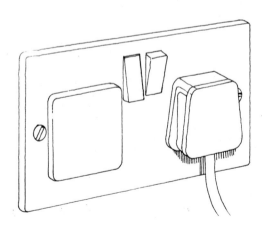

Emergency locks: Discourage children from using the locks on bathroom and toilet doors. If possible replace existing locks with the kind that can be opened from the outside in an emergency.

Bathroom locks: If a child locks him or herself in the bathroom and can't get out, distract his or her attention by passing a favourite comic under the door. Many bathroom locks can be opened with a minimum of damage by levering the frame and the door apart at the point where the bolt enters the frame. If this doesn't work you can try shouldering the door – but remember to tell the child to stand well clear. If this, too, fails call a locksmith or, finally, dial 999. (See Emergency Locks above.)

Plastic bags: Never leave plastic bags within the reach of children.

Electric flex: Don't let animals or children play with flexes, they are easy to bite through.

Pond netting: If you have very small children about, fix netting over all ponds and pools – even ornamental ones. A small child can drown in only a few inches of water.

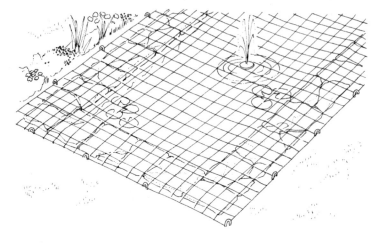

Glass stickers: Children often cannot see whether an all-glass patio door is open or closed until it's too late. To help them, stick something on the glass at their eye level.

Babysitters: When using a babysitter, give her a list of what to do if a fire breaks out, the telephone rings, someone comes to the door, she smells gas, the fuses go, or a child becomes ill. You should also leave her the telephone number of the place you are going to.

It's no bother: If a child is late home inform the police if this is in any way abnormal. Don't be afraid of 'bothering' the police. They never mind being alerted unnecessarily.

Friend not foe: Never give your children any cause to be frightened of the police. They may need a policeman's help at some stage, but they will not go to him if they think he is a bogey-man.

Delayed reactions: If you pick your child up from school consider the consequences if you are delayed for any reason. If you know you are going to be late 'phone the school secretary. If possible make an advance arrangement for another mother to pick your child up, you can do the same for her when needed.

Strange stories: When warning your children about going with strangers don't forget that the stories used may not be obvious. For instance, what would your child do if told that what they were doing was 'very naughty' and they were to get in the car – the person was going to take them home and tell their mummy about it?

PERSONAL SAFETY

Slipping rugs: Never polish the floor under a rug. If you have a small rug that tends to slither about dangerously on a polished floor, hold it in place by brushing strips of latex adhesive around the edges. Leave this to dry before replacing the rug.

Razor blades: Press one edge of a double-sided razor blade into the disused match stub end of a bookmatch. It will protect your fingers when you use it.

Pins and needles: Don't hold pins and needles in your mouth while sewing or put them in your clothes – use a pincushion.

Waxed floors: When waxing floors make sure you apply the wax thinly and evenly. An uneven, or too thick, coating of wax will cause accidents. For similar reasons never wax uncarpeted stairs.

Many a slip: Roughen the soles of slippery footwear with sandpaper to avoid accidents.

Slippery soles: Crêpe soles, from which the tread has worn, can be very slippery in wet or greasy conditions. You can renew the tread by cutting shallow V-shaped grooves across the soles with a razor blade.

Dark stairs: Many bad falls are caused when somebody has to come up or down stairs in the dark. Avoid them by getting two way switches fitted.

Toys: It's not just in cartoons that someone steps on a roller skate and glides through a window to end up in hospital. Train your children to pick up toys straight after playing with them, and don't let them play on the stairs.

... and pets: Pets can be the source of many a nasty fall, too – don't let them get into the habit of lying in doorways or across stairs.

Sharp objects: Remember that what you throw away can be a hazard to dustmen – never throw out anything sharp (razor blades, broken glass, etc.) without first wrapping it in newspaper. If you are throwing away a large amount of broken glass (from a window, say) it is essential to warn the dustmen about it.

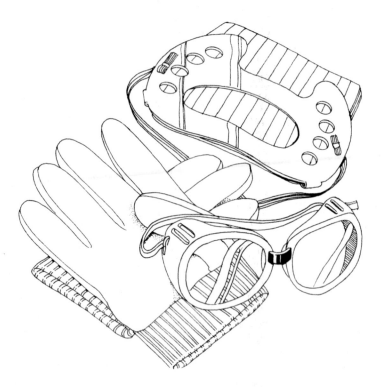

Safe D.I.Y.: Strong gardening gloves are ideal for protecting your hands when working with heavy tools. When drilling or chiselling at brick work or tiling, always wear safety glasses to protect your eyes. Any job that involves a lot of dust can be a danger to your lungs – protect them with a mask obtainable from chemists.

Important labels: D.I.Y. tools and preparations have become very sophisticated and therefore potentially dangerous in recent years. Don't take risks – read through the instructions fully before starting to use them.

Mixed chemicals: Never mix two chemicals together – poisonous fumes often result.

Harmful fumes: Many products, particularly cleaning fluids, emit fumes that are harmful. The effect is often cumulative, that is, the substance enters the body and is not dispersed, so that each small exposure to the chemical adds up to what can in some cases be a lethal dose. Therefore before using any product that gives off fumes or vapours or smells strongly, or has a warning on the packet, open all the windows in a room, then try to avoid breathing the fumes directly.

Hidden poisons: Manufacturers are not always obliged by law to declare that their products are poisonous. For example after-shave, carpet cleaners, detergents, disinfectants, dyes, lavatory cleaners, perfumes, shampoos and white spirit all are, or contain, poisons. They are all safe if used correctly, but should be kept out of the reach of young children.

The right steps: If you are hanging curtains or getting something out of a high cupboard, use a set of steps rather than a chair, which you could tip up. Wear flat shoes, too, otherwise your heels may catch in your hem.

No clocks or mirrors: It is not a good idea to hang a clock or a mirror over the fireplace. People then tend to stand too close to the fire in order to look at them and are in danger of being burnt.

Kitchen curtains: Don't hang curtains at your kitchen window if the cooker is beside it. They may catch fire if they flap when the window is open. A blind is a better idea.

Kitchen sockets: If you are planning to put in new sockets above your work surface in the kitchen, they should be at least 23 cm (10 inches) above the surface and not too near the water source.

Poisonous plants: Some house plants are poisonous – find out whether any of yours are; if so, label them clearly to enable you to identify them in an emergency.

Spray paints: When using aerosol spray paints indoors, be sure to open the windows before you start.

HYGIENE

Natural bristles: Don't use a natural bristle toothbrush. The bristles are hollow and may therefore collect minute food particles which will allow germs to breed.

Tin opening: When opening tin cans remember to wipe over the top with a damp cloth first – this will remove any dust and grease that may have accumulated and stop this getting into the food. Don't try to open a tin when the bottom is resting on a slippery surface – put a damp cloth underneath to keep it steady.

Scrubbable surfaces: When planning a kitchen or bathroom remember that all the surfaces should be scrubbable. Surfaces that are cracked should be repaired since the cracks provide an ideal place for germs to breed in.

Clean grouting: Although wall tiles will be left clean after a quick wipe with a damp cloth, the grouting between tiles will need a good scrub to keep it clean.

Hidden dirt: The dirt and grease that tends to accumulate around, and particularly behind, cookers tends to be missed out in the ordinary process of cleaning. However, this can be highly flammable as well as unhygienic, so make a point of removing it regularly. You may find that there are other places where dust and dirt collect that tend to be missed out; give these a good scrub at the same time.

Dry food storage: Although dry foods will not go off if left in contact with air, they should be stored in sealed containers to keep them safe from insects and vermin.

Meat: Raw meat and cooked meat should always be kept separate. Don't buy either from a butcher who keeps the two together. If you have to keep both in the fridge at the same time, make sure that they are kept well wrapped on the same shelf (if they are kept on different shelves the juices from one may drip on to the other). After cutting raw meat on a board, always scrub it carefully and disinfect with a little bleach before using it for anything else.

Clean seat: It's important to make sure the toilet and the toilet seat are kept clean. Because of their size children have to hoist themselves up on to the seat, and are therefore likely to pick up germs from it.

Personal gear: To restrict the way in which minor (and major) ailments are transmitted to all members of the family, make sure that everybody has his or her own personal flannel, toothbrush and towels. If you have young children, encourage them to stick to using their own things by buying a complete set for each of them in a matching colour.

Cover cuts: When preparing food, keep your hands clean and cover any cuts or sores with sticking plaster. If an existing dressing is dirty, change it before starting to cook.

Dust and germs: Dust from a vacuum cleaner should be wrapped carefully in old newspaper and disposed of in a dustbin, not a wastebin. This dust contains millions of germs which, if allowed to get into the air, can cause infections of the lungs, as well as asthma attacks.

Prompt eating: Foods should be eaten within two days of their 'sell-by' dates.

Pet food: Try not to leave half-eaten bowls of cat or dog food lying around. These will attract flies.

First aid

GENERAL HINTS

Hospital in a hurry: If someone has to be got to hospital in a hurry and he or she can be moved easily, it is often quicker, if you have a car, to take the person yourself rather than call for an ambulance.

Broken bones: If you suspect that someone has broken a bone, don't attempt to move him or make him stand, call a hospital – the same rules apply to suspected internal injuries.

Electrocution: One of the effects that large amounts of electricity have on the body is to operate the muscles. This means that in some cases a person may become stuck to what they are touching – their muscles tighten up and do not allow them to let go. *Do not touch them* or you will receive a shock as well. Instead turn the electricity off at the source. If this is not possible push the person clear with a piece of wood. Be careful when moving someone who has been shocked – the electricity may have operated muscles together that normally only work in opposition (in the upper arm for example). This places great strain on bones and can break them.

No food: If someone has injured him or herself in such a way as to lead you to think an anaesthetic might be needed (a broken leg or arm, for example) don't give him or her anything to eat or drink while waiting for the ambulance. If you do, it will mean that he or she cannot be given an anaesthetic for several hours.

Shock: If a person is suffering from shock after an accident, keep him warm by covering him with a blanket. Stay with him and give plenty of reassurance – send someone else for an ambulance.

Reassured but awake: A person suffering from shock should not be allowed to fall asleep.

Curing cramp: Cramp is caused by a lack of oxygen in the blood supplied to a muscle. Anything that improves the blood supply will cure it – the application of a towel dipped in warm water, rubbing or exercising. A stitch is a cramp of the diaphragm, the cure (and the way to avoid getting a stitch) is to breath in a regular and controlled way.

MEDICINES AND FIRST AID KIT

Old medicine: When you finish a course of treatment of a prescribed medicine, don't put the bottle with any remaining tablets back in the cupboard – flush the tablets or medicine down the lavatory and throw the bottle away.

Medicine safety: Although it may be difficult to get young children to take medicine, never tell them tablets are sweets – they may take you at your word and help themselves to more of them.

Uses for bicarbonate: Keep some bicarbonate of soda in your medicine box: it can be used for treating scalds and mild burns (make up a paste with water), as a treatment for heartburn (drink a pinch in a glass of hot water), and as a gargle for sore throats.

Taking a pill: When swallowing a pill the trick, to avoid tasting it, is not to let it touch your tongue. You can do this by resting it on the back of your lower front teeth, taking a gulp of water and swallowing it down with the water. A child can suck an ice lolly before taking an unpleasant medicine. This will numb the taste buds for a short time and is also a reward for having to take something nasty.

245

First aid kit: Keep the following in your first aid box:
  1 roll of porous surgical tape
  2 large and 2 medium prepared wound dressings
  1 packet sterilized cotton wool
  2 tubular gauze bandages
  2 large triangular bandages
  1 standard crêpe bandage
  the doctor's telephone number
  tweezers
  an eye bath
  a sharp needle, sterilized
  safety pins
  scissors

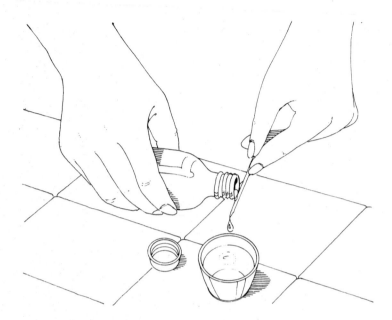

Limited drops: Where medicine requires that you administer a certain number of drops, you can do so accurately by holding a toothpick across the top of the bottle and running the medicine down the length of this.

Timely reminder: When a medicine needs to be taken at rigidly fixed times, use a kitchen timer or an alarm clock to remind you.

No swapping: Never give a medicine prescribed for one person to another, no matter how similar their symptoms seem. Also, never save the remnants of a medicine to treat yourself if the illness recurs.

BURNS AND SCALDS

Clothing on fire: A person whose clothes are on fire should be rolled in a rug, blanket, or piece of carpet. This will stop air getting to the flames and so put out the fire.

Blisters: When treating burns beware of bursting blisters. These become infected very easily and can lead to major complications.

Scalding: Remove any tight fitting clothes from a person who has been scalded (do not do this for someone who has been burnt). Scalding causes swelling and clothing will cause painful constrictions.

No butter: Don't put butter on burns – if they are serious leave well alone and call a doctor. Mild burns should be treated by holding them under cold running water for 5–10 minutes.

Mild burns: The freshly cut surface of an onion can bring relief from mild burns and stings.

Small burns: Painful, but small, burns on hands can be relieved by soaking in water containing a few dissolved aspirins.

FITS, FEVER AND FAINTING

Fits: Don't restrict the movements of a person suffering a fit. Loosen his clothing if it is tight, but do not attempt to put anything in his mouth. Put something soft under his neck. When the fit is over do not move him, let him lie still until he has time to work out where he is.

Fever: Treat a person suffering from a fever with aspirin (the dose recommended for someone of her age). If her temperature is particularly high, sponge her with tepid water (the cooling effect comes from allowing the water to evaporate).

Fainting: Fainting is caused by a lack of oxygen in the blood supplied to the brain. Loosen tight clothing, give the patient plenty of space and, if the room is hot, or smoky, open the windows. To rouse him you must increase the amount of blood going to the head. Do this by putting his head

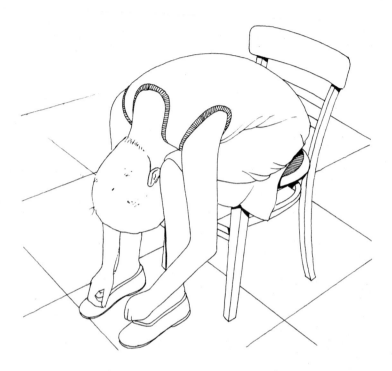

between his knees if he is sitting. If he falls to the ground, raise his legs up above the level of his head. Don't try to pick him up – fainting is to some extent a protective measure, since if a person is lying down more blood is going to his head anyway.

FEET

Cutting toenails: Toenails should always be cut straight across, rather than following the shape of the toe. This will prevent them from ingrowing.

Foam lining: Wellington boots transfer the shock of walking to the foot and, as well as tiring the walker, are very cold in winter. A solution is to slip a piece of foam rubber cut to the shape of the foot into each boot.

FOREIGN BODIES

Something in the eye: Most of the time when someone complains of something in his or her eye it will not be on the surface of the eye but on the inside of the lid. It can be removed by pulling the eyelid back, twisting the corner of a clean handkerchief to a point and using this to dab the object off the lid. If there is something stuck to the eye itself, do not attempt to remove it – get medical help.

Splinters: Do not attempt to remove glass splinters or any splinters lodged under a nail – see a doctor and get him to take them out.

Removing splinters: To get a splinter out without trouble, place the effected area of skin over the top of a bottle or jar filled with very hot water. Keep the skin in firm contact with the bottle top. The heat and pressure will push the splinter out.

Choking: Don't panic when dealing with someone who is choking – your panic will be transmitted and cause him or her to constrict his or her throat around the blockage. With serious cases, get medical help straightaway or go directly to the nearest hospital casualty department.

Choking and small children: Small children or babies who are choking can be treated by hanging them upside down and firmly patting their backs to dislodge the object. However, if they seem to be choking very badly, just get them to hospital straightaway.

DAY TO DAY PROBLEMS

Bruises: The pain and the look of bruises can be relieved by applying a little dry starch moistened with water to the area as soon as possible after the injury takes place.

Boils: To draw the core out of a boil, make a poultice as follows: mix together one spoon each of honey, oil and flour, beat a yoke of egg into this and spread on a piece of gauze. Apply to the boil overnight.

Nose bleeds: Nose bleeds only need medical treatment if they last longer than twenty minutes, or if the sufferer is an old person.

Large cuts: Do not apply any material directly to any large cut when you are not sure whether it contains any foreign material (glass, etc.). Instead use clean material around, but not touching, the wound while you wait for the ambulance.

Stings: A bee's sting contains muscles that continue to work after the sting has been detached from the bee. These allow the sting to actually dig its way into the skin, and then to inject the poison into the wound. The trick therefore in removing a sting is to get it out as quickly as you can. Use the edge of a fingernail in a scraping motion to remove it. A wasp's sting is different. The damage is done once it has stung you – no sting is left to be removed.

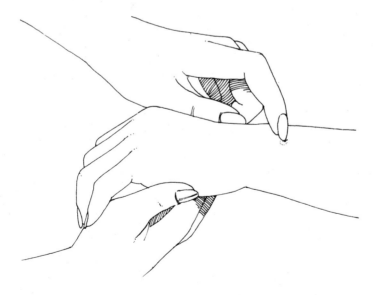

Hangover cure: Most of the effects of a hangover are the result of the dehydration that alcohol causes. It can be prevented by drinking two or three glasses of water before going to bed.

Headache cure: Headaches triggered by foods and drinks which are the products of fermentation can be cured, if they are not severe, with a hot drink of milk and honey.

Expanding the chest: Any kind of activity which involves blowing will expand the chest cavity and therefore be good for a child who suffers from asthma – try bubble blowing, blow football, etc.

Toothache: A clove dipped in a little whisky or brandy and applied to the affected area will provide temporary relief from a toothache.

Poisoning: A person suffering from any kind of poisoning should be taken to hospital as quickly as possible – take a sample of the poison with you if you have it. Don't try to make them sick, don't give them anything to eat or drink, except if they complain of burning of the throat or mouth, in which case give them plenty of water, but nothing else. Never give anything to a person who is unconscious. If someone is poisoned make a note of the time you discover them – this will help the hospital decide on treatment.

Earache: Some relief can be given to a person suffering from earache by keeping the ear warm – use a hot water bottle or warm oil dripped into the ear and retained with a plug of cotton wool.

HEALTH AND SAFETY RECORD

Keep a list of emergency phone numbers as a handy record in case of accidents.

Doctor ....

Dentist ....

School ....

Local police station ....

Gas emergency ....

Electricity emergency ....

It is also useful to keep a record of details of the family's health. Whoever takes the children to the doctor will need to have information on infectious diseases, especially if the G.P. is new to you.

Name ....

Injections ....

Infectious diseases ....

Hospital treatment ....

Blood group ....

Any allergies? ....

Name ....

Injections ....

Infectious diseases ....

Hospital treatment ....

Blood group ....

Any allergies? ....

"Waste Not, Want Not"

**Metric conversion
charts of useful measures**

SEWING AND KNITTING MATERIALS

Knitting needles and crochet hooks have both gone over to metric sizing. The old and new sizes are compared below.

Knitting needles		Crochet hooks (wool)	
Old size	Metric size	Old size	Metric size
000	10	2	7 mm
00	9	4	6 mm
0	8	5	5.50 mm
1	7½ (7.5)	6	5 mm
2	7	7	4.50 mm
3	6½ (6.5)	8	4 mm
4	6	9	3.50 mm
5	5½ (5.5)	10	3 mm
6	5	12	2.50 mm
7	4½ (4.5)	14	2 mm
8	4	Crochet hooks (cotton)	
9	3¾ (3.75)	1½	2 mm
10	3¼ (3.25)	2½	1.75 mm
11	3	3½	1.50 mm
12	2¾ (2.75)	4½	1.25 mm
13	2¼ (2.25)	5½	1.00 mm
14	2	6½	0.75 mm
		7	0.60 mm

SCREWS AND SCREW SIZES

Below are some suggested guide-hole diameters for standard wood screws. They are only a guide: the holes may need to be slightly larger in hardwood or smaller in softwood.

Screw	Point hole	Shank hole
No. 4	2.0 mm	2.5 mm
No. 6	2.5 mm	3.5 mm
No. 8	3.0 mm	4.5 mm
No. 10	3.5 mm	5.0 mm
No. 12	4.0 mm	5.5 mm
No. 14	4.5 mm	6.5 mm

The following is a list of typical jobs for standard-gauge screws:

No. 4 Very small cabinet hinges, keyhole-cover plates.

No. 6 Window hinges, curtain rail brackets, door handles, lock-sets.

No. 8 Door hinges, light-duty shelf brackets, general box-construction.

No. 10 Heavier shelf brackets, wall-cupboard mountings, hinges for heavy doors.

No. 12 Adjustable, slotted-steel, heavy-duty shelf systems, small-to-medium central-heating radiators, wall-mounted boilers, outdoor trellis supports.

No. 14 Heavy and double-size central-heating radiators, shelf brackets for heavy loads, sturdy frame construction (benches, tables, and so on).

Metric equivalents of screw sizes are as follows:

millimetres	9	12	15	19	25	32	38	44	50	57	63	76	89	101
inches	$3/8$	$1/2$	$5/8$	$3/4$	1	$1 1/4$	$1 1/2$	$1 3/4$	2	$2 1/4$	$2 1/2$	3	$3 1/2$	4

CHILDREN'S CLOTHING

Below is a general guide to metric and imperial measurements and sizing.

	Age	Weight	Chest	Height
*	3 months	5.5 kg/12 lb		62 cm/24½"
*	6 months	8 kg/18 lb		69 cm/27"
*	9 months	9.5 kg/21 lb		74 cm/29"
*	12 months	11 kg/24 lb		79 cm/31"
†	18 months	12.5 kg/28 lb		83 cm/33"
†	2 years		51 cm/20¼"	92 cm/36"
†	3 years		53 cm/20⅞"	98 cm/38"
†	4 years		55 cm/21½"	104 cm/40"

* clothes marked by weight/age
† clothes marked by height/age

MEN'S CLOTHING

Collar sizes

inches	14½	15	15½	16	16½	17	17½
cm	37	38	39/40	41	42	43	44

Waist measurements

inches	26	28	30	32	34	36	38	40	42
cm	66	71	76	81	86	91	97	102	107

SHOE SIZES

The three series of measurements do not exactly correspond, so you may need to try one or two sizes before getting the right fit. American sizes apply only to women's shoes.

British	American	Continental
3	4½ (45)	36
4	5½ (55)	37
5	6½ (65)	38
		39
6	7½ (75)	40
7	8½ (85)	41
8	9½ (95)	42
9		43
		44
10		45
11		46

WOMEN'S CLOTHING

Size	inches bust/hip	cm bust/hip
8	30/32	76/81
10	32/34	81/86
12	34/36	86/91
14	36/38	91/97
16	38/40	97/102
18	40/42	102/107
20	42/44	107/112
22	44/46	112/117
24	46/48	117/122

WEIGHTS AND MEASURES

The exact conversion of 1 oz to 28.349 grams makes exact calculation too complicated for practical weighing, so the Metrication Board suggests that 1 oz is taken as 25 grams for amounts under 1 lb, and 30 grams for amounts over 1 lb.

This is a rough guide, showing approximate equivalents.

1 oz	2 oz	3 oz	4 oz	8 oz
25 g	50 g	75 g	100 g	200 g

When weighing amounts in excess of 1 lb:

1 lb	2 lb	3 lb	4 lb	5 lb
450 g	900 g	1½ kg	1¾ kg	2¼ kg

LIQUIDS

The litre is the basic unit for measurement in metric. It is approximately equivalent to 1¾ pints. 4½ litres are about equal to 1 gallon.

Below are rough equivalents in pints of buying ⅛, ¼, ½ and whole litres.

¼ pint	½ pint	1 pint	2 pints
150 ml	300 ml	600 ml	1200 ml

SPOONS

¼ teaspoon	1.25 millilitres
½ teaspoon	2.5 millilitres
1 teaspoon	5 millilitres
1 tablespoon	15 millilitres

MEASURING LENGTH

The metre is the basic unit for measurement in metric. It is just over 3¼ feet. The following are exact equivalents:

1 inch = 25.4 millimetres

1 foot = 0.3048 metres

1 yard = 0.9144 metres

1 mile = 1.6093 kilometres

1 millimetre = 0.394 inches

1 centimetre = 0.3937 inches

1 metre = 39.37 inches

1 kilometre = 0.6214 miles

On the right, however, is a handy guide to show you at a glance how the two systems compare:

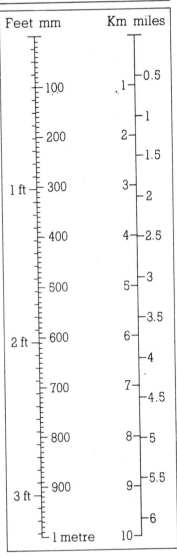

TEMPERATURES

Most temperatures are now measured in Celsius, formerly Centigrade. To convert Fahrenheit to Celsius, subtract 32, multiply by 5, divide by 9. This gives an approximate figure. To convert Celsius into Fahrenheit, multiply by 9, divide by 5, add 32. Normal body temperature (formerly 98.6°F) is now measured as 37°C. Normal room temperature for central heating is 18°C for the bedroom and 22°C for the living room. The tables opposite show conversions for the range of temperatures used for the oven/freezer (left) and for outdoors (right). Below is a guide to electric and gas oven temperatures.

OVEN TEMPERATURES

Centigrade		Fahrenheit	Gas mark
100	very cool	200	Low
110		225	1/4
120		250	1/2
140	cool	275	1
150		300	2
160	moderate	325	3
180		350	4
190	mod. hot	375	5
200		400	6
220	hot	425	7
230		450	8
240	very hot	475	9
260		500	10

FAHRENHEIT/CELSIUS CONVERSIONS

Oven/Freezer

Fahrenheit	Celsius
0	−17.7 deep freeze
water freezes 32	0
50	10
	20
	30
100	40
	50
	60
150	70
	80
200	90
212	100
	110
250	120
	130
	140
300	150
	160
	170
350	180
	190
	200
400	210
	220
450	230
	240
	250
500	260

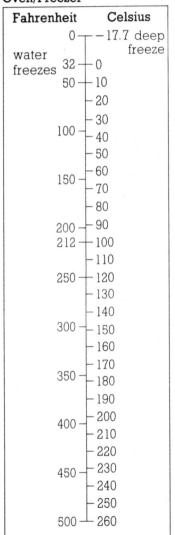

Outdoors

Fahrenheit	Celsius	
0		
	−15	
10		
	−10	
20		
	−5	
32 30	0	freezing
40	5	
50	10	cool
60	15	mild
70	20	warm
	25	very warm
80		
	30	hot
90	35	
98.6 100	37	body temp.
	40	
110	45	
120	50	

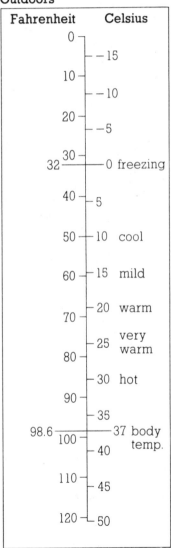

BEDS AND BED LINEN

Sizes of bedding can be confusing now that they are all metricated. Below is a chart showing what sizes will fit what size of bed. Variations allow for different mattress thicknesses and tuck-in allowances.

Bed type	Bed size	
Single	90 cm × 190 cm	3′×6′3″
Large single	100 cm × 200 cm	3′3″×6′6″
Double	135 cm × 190 cm	4′6″×6′3″
Large double	150 cm × 200 cm	5′×6′6″

Bed type	Blanket size	
Single	180 cm × 240 cm	5′11″×7′11″
Large single	200 cm × 250 cm	6′6″×8′
Double	230 cm × 250 cm	7′6″×8′
Large double	260 cm × 250 cm	8′6″×8′
Extra large	300 cm × 250 cm	10′×8′

Bed type	Blended sheets	Cotton & flannelette sheets
Single	175 cm × 260 cm 5′9″×8′6″	175 cm × 255 cm to 275 cm 5′9″×8′5″ to 9′ 200 cm × 255 cm to 275 cm 6′6″×8′5″ to 9′
Large single	175 cm × 260 cm 5′9″×8′6″	175 cm × 275 cm 5′9″×9′ 200 cm × 275 cm 6′6″×9′
Double	230 cm × 260 cm 7′6″×8′6″	230 cm × 255 cm to 275 cm 7′6″×8′5″ to 9′
Large double	230 cm × 260 cm 7′6″×8′6″	230 cm × 275 cm 7′6″×9′
Extra large	275 cm × 275 cm 9′×9′	270 cm × 295 cm 8′11″×9′8″

MOTORING

Tyre pressures, as well as petrol pumps, have also come in for metrication. The following two tables show rough equivalents.

Petrol measures		Tyre pressures	
litres	gallons	lb/sq in	kg/cm²
5	1.1	10	0.7
10	2.2	12	0.8
15	3.3	15	1.1
20	4.4	18	1.3
25	5.5	20	1.4
30	6.6	21	1.5
35	7.7	23	1.6
40	8.8	24	1.7
45	9.9	26	1.8
50	11.0	27	1.9
		28	2.0
		30	2.1
		33	2.3
		36	2.5
		38	2.7
		40	2.8

"Many Hands Make Light Work"

Where to turn for help and advice

Services

BUILDING

Building regulations: There are various building regulations which can restrict you in terms of what you can do to your home. Your local Town Hall Building Control Department will be happy to give you, free of charge, advice as to what you can and cannot do if you are planning to improve, change or extend your house in some way.

Planning permission: Apart from Building Regulations approval (which ensures that work is carried out safely and to certain standards), you may need planning permission for your new playroom, verandah, swimming pool or sauna, which governs the appearance of the structure on the environment. Check with the Planning Department (at the local borough or district council offices).

Impartial advice: The Building Centre in London at 26 Store Street, WC1 (and in Scotland at 3 Claremont Terrace, Glasgow G3) can put you wise about everything from the sort of bricks you might use to the best way to ventilate the chimney. No charge is made. If you don't live near London or Glasgow, you can always telephone your query to the centre nearest you.

Heating systems: While the various fuel suppliers will advise about heating systems (and probably each claim theirs is the best), you can get impartial advice by writing to the Heating Centre, (The Institute of Domestic Heating Engineers), 77 New Bond Street, London W1Y 9DB. The centre does charge for this though, so check on this first.

CRIME PREVENTION

Police advice: All police forces have a crime prevention officer who will go round your house and advise you how best to protect it and its contents. Ring the station to arrange an appointment. Usually there are leaflets they can leave with you too.

Neighbourly help: Good neighbour schemes operate in some areas and as part of the scheme someone could check your house regularly if you're away from home. No charge would be made. Your local police station is the place to ask for details of any such scheme.

Spot checks: Police can't physically protect your property if you're away from home – they don't have the manpower. However, if your house is to be empty for long periods, leave a note about this at your local station and if it's possible they will ask the local beat bobby to make a spot check now and then to see if all's safe and well. Again, no charge.

Extra protection: If you need greater protection, then a private security firm should be contacted. They'll charge for their services of course.

ELECTRICITY AND GAS

Supply failure: If your electricity supply falters and you establish first that there's no general power cut in the area, and secondly that all your fuses are intact, then call your local electricity board to send someone out. In a rural area particularly, there can sometimes be a fault at the point where the overhead line brings the supply into your property. The service to mend a fault in the supply will be free, but if your domestic wiring is at fault, a charge will be made.

Check consumption: Would you like to know how many units the toaster or the TV uses? Your local electricity board showroom will be able to tell you and also supply you with leaflets which detail the consumption of every sort of appliance from blenders to battery chargers. Leaflets on the running costs of gas appliances and central heating are also available at gas region showrooms.

Check the meter: Is the electricity or gas meter whizzing round at an alarming rate? If you think there might be something wrong with it, call your local electricity board or gas region and they will arrange to have it checked out. There may be a charge.

Moving: When you move into a new house or leave your old one, the local electricity board and local gas region will send someone out to read the meter. No charge will be made.

Leaks: The moment you think there's a gas leak, turn off all appliances and the meter, extinguish all cigarettes and naked flames, and open doors and windows. Don't turn any electric switches on or off. Then call your gas emergency number – it's in the directory under 'GAS' – who will send someone out as soon as they can. No charge for the first 30 minutes' work including parts up to the value of £1.

Difficulties: Those who are elderly or handicapped and find difficulty operating domestic appliances using gas or electricity can get in touch with the local gas regions or electricity boards and a home economist will visit them and advise about ways in which operation of the appliances might be made easier. No charge is made.

FIRE

999: When there's any fire about – whether it's straw burning in a nearby field which looks as though it might spread to houses or you set the chip pan alight – call the Fire Brigade by dialling 999.

Prevention: If you have worries about how safe your house would be in the event of a fire give your local Fire Prevention Office a ring and ask for advice. If you have any worries about fire precautions, such as which type of extinguisher to

buy and so on, again the local Fire Brigade will usually advise
you. All extinguishers should comply with British Standard
4547 or be included in the 'List of Approved Portable Fire
Extinguishing Appliances' published by the Fire Offices'
Committee (such extinguishers are marked to that effect).

Extra services: Emergencies in the home, such as young
Timmy sticking his head in the garden railings or the cat
getting stuck up a twenty foot tree, will also be dealt with by
the Fire Brigade, probably free of charge. The policy does
vary from one area to another. The brigade can, in fact, make
a charge for any service other than putting out fires but most
don't usually do so where life and limb is threatened.

IMPROVEMENT GRANTS

Grants for improving property: Local authorities can provide various grants to householders – for the improvement
of the property in some way or another. The conditions
attached to the grants can vary.

Standard Amenities Grant: This one is mandatory and covers
such things as the installation of a bathroom, kitchen sink and
larder facilities.

Improvement Grant – Discretionary: Given for improving
existing houses or for converting houses or other buildings.

Improvement Grants for Houses in Housing Action Areas:
These are given in an area where the council has decided
that some houses must be demolished and others need to be
brought up to a specified standard.

Repairs Grant: For houses requiring repairs which, if neg-
lected, would threaten the future life of a house and the cost of
which would cause the owner hardship.

Insulation Grant: Where you have no insulation at all in the
attic or round water pipes, the local authority will pay a
proportion of the cost.

Replacement of Lead Plumbing Grant: This is for replacing certain lead pipes which carry drinking water – sometimes only given if there is a high percentage of lead in the water – sometimes given automatically, depending on the council.

IN THE GARDEN

Getting advice: Most local authority offices will be more than willing to give you free advice on all sorts of gardening problems. They can advise you which varieties of flowers and shrubs are best suited to the local soil; how to cope with everything from greenfly to grubs; how to perk up your soil. The actual service varies from one authority to another and indeed even the department which gives it can vary.

Demonstrations: Often there are what are called 'demonstration gardens', where local authority gardeners show you how to do all sorts of tasks from pruning roses to propagating pansies: all for free. Usually these demonstrations are held regularly throughout the year and are advertised in local papers. Other authorities have a number you can phone to get answers to your garden queries, and if you are very lucky, and your local authority has a special interest in gardening, you might even get someone coming along to your garden to advise you. Again, at no charge.

Tree trouble: First port of call should be your local council. Many of them will help you identify pests and quite a number have arboricultural officers who will visit your garden and tell you whether trees are dangerous or not, whether they need pruning, and so on. And even those authorities which don't run to that, will at least be able to give you a list of local contractors who will prune or, if necessary, fell trees.

LAW

Citizens Advice Bureau: If you have any queries on how the law affects your family, your property, tenants, rights or which benefits or social services are available, the local Citizens' Advice Bureau is the place to go for help. If they cannot provide the answer, they will certainly point you in the direction of someone who can. If there is no CAB near enough to your home for you to call in personally, you can telephone with your query. Citizens' Advice Bureaux offer free, confidential, impartial and independent advice and information on any subject.

PESTS

Bats: Since the 1981 Countryside Act came in it's been illegal to get rid of or block the access of bats. The law doesn't mean, though, that you are likely to be stuck with the bats for ever or until they decide to move on. What you do is contact your nearest branch of the Nature Conservancy Council. They will send someone along and, when they consider the time to be right, will move (not destroy) the furry creatures. You may have to wait some months, if it's the breeding season for instance. Look for the Council in your local phone book and if there doesn't seem to be a nearby branch, contact their headquarters at 19–20 Belgrave Square, London SW1. They do not make a charge.

Woodworm and dry rot: There's no free service available to get rid of these beetles or prevent them attacking your timbers in the future but you will be able to get a free quotation from professional firms who deal with this problem. And, since it is free, get as many estimates from different firms as you can. There can be a quite amazing difference between what one charges and another. Shop around and do choose one which gives you a twenty year guarantee. This can be useful, not just for your own peace of mind, but when you sell the house you can proudly display your certificate.

Rats and mice: These vermin can often be dealt with by the householder but a positive plague of them can be hard to handle. Environmental health departments of local authorities are usually prepared to give you advice on how to get rid of pests and they may do it for you (but this is purely a matter for their discretion, you can't demand this service as a ratepayer). Your other option is to pay for the professionals to do the job. The British Pest Control Association at Alembic House, 93 Albert Embankment, London SE1 will give you a list of local firms. Ask for a quotation before you book them.

Wasps: Wasps' nests should be left to the experts, unless you have specialized knowledge yourself. Most local authorities do have facilities for dealing with wasps' nests but they are likely to make a charge. Pest control firms will also deal with nests.

Cockroaches, fleas and lice: If DIY treatment doesn't seem to be having much effect, you'll find a sympathetic ear at your local council offices. Depending on where you live – you could get advice or someone to treat the problem, and often no charge will be made.

Bees: Honey bees can often escape from hives and swarm all around someone else's house or garden; they may even like the idea of setting up home in it and build a nest. These are not strictly speaking pests, just a nuisance. If you find yourself in the middle of a swarm, don't start swatting, contact a local bee keeper. If you don't know any, then ask the police or the local authority who may keep a list of names for emergencies such as yours. No charge.

REFUSE

Local rules: Although the local authority agrees to pick up your empty tins and household leftovers they can insist that you put them in a particular type of container: it could be a bin, a bag or whatever. If they require you, for instance, to use paper or plastic sacks, they can decide how many free sacks each household is entitled to and that you must buy any extra you need. The authority can also dictate where you leave your rubbish for collection – i.e. at the front of the house, at the back, by the kerbside or whatever.

Remote rubbish: Remote areas could have problems with rubbish, so bear this in mind before you move to the top of a mountain! Councils don't have a statutory duty to collect remote rubbish. However, if they prove stubborn on the point, contact the Secretary of State for Environment, he can require the local authority to provide a service.

Tips: Any old bedsteads and suchlike – even your old cars – can be disposed of free of charge at local depots or 'tips', which local authorities have a duty to provide. Of course they don't have a duty to provide one near you, they will be located at a suitable site, and that might be many miles away. Your local Town Hall will give details of where such depots are.

Hire a skip: Alternatively, if facilities for 'medium size' household rubbish are few and far between, get together with a group of neighbours and ask your council if they could provide a skip in your area. Watch out, though: skips can bring a lot of mess and broken bottles and litter all over the place! Another point to bear in mind about skips is that, if you don't have space to put one inside your own boundaries, you will have to ask the local planning department for permission to site it on the pavement or roadway and it must be well lit at night.

Eyesores: If someone parks their old banger near your house and the local vandals start stripping off the wheels and then the doors and then the kids start playing in it and you get angrier and angrier because it's proving such an eyesore, get in touch with your local environmental health department. They are usually quite sympathetic to the abandoned car problem and will probably try to find the owner of the car or remove it themselves.

Large scale rubbish: Getting a new fridge or washing machine or whatever is lovely but what do you do with the old one? In spite of the fact that some people seem to think the only thing you can do is dump them on the nearest bit of open countryside, there is a simple answer! Once again, your local environmental health department will come to the rescue. Almost all of them, wherever you live, will call and collect these larger household items but you may have to wait until the regular collection day in your area, so be patient. Usually this service is free, but it may vary and some authorities may make a small charge, especially if they have to make a special trip.

Bottle banks: Many local councils have set up 'bottle banks' in car parks or near to large stores and all you have to do is pop in your empties. The bottle bank service is quite free to the public and in fact it can even help to plough money back into the community because the scheme is usually operated in conjunction with one of the large glass companies and they pay for the glass they get from the banks. Ring your district council to check whether there's one in your area.

Rubble: Rubble can ruin your garden – you can't expect the refuse collectors to take it away and if you were simply to slip a shovelful of it at a time into your bin or bag it would probably take years to clear the stuff! There are two alternatives. Some local authorities (roughly half) will take it away for you free. The alternative is to hire a skip (see page 275).

TELEPHONE

Faults: Repairing faults on your line is a free service from British Telecom. And if the fault isn't repaired two days after it has been reported, you can apply to the Customer Service division of your local telephone area for a pro rata rebate.

Costs: If you want to check up on how much you've spent on phone calls and the bill's not due for a bit you can have a special meter reading. Contact your local area telephone office and ask for it. There will be a small charge for this service.

Meters: You can in fact rent a meter for an annual charge (check the current charge with your local Telecom office). However, it's claimed that there are possible line conditions which could interfere with the operation of your home based meter, so it won't necessarily compare exactly with the meter used to calculate your bill. But there shouldn't be huge discrepancies and it would certainly make a worthwhile comparison point if you feel your bills are always too high.

Number change: If you are constantly getting calls for the local pub because the number's similar, you can get your number changed – at the price of a few pounds.

Moving house: When you move to a new house and a new phone number, there may still be some people trying to get in touch with you at your previous number. While the old number is covered by rental you have already paid, the operator will tell callers your new number for no charge. But that's likely to be a very limited time – after that you can arrange for an 'interception on a ceased line' service from British Telecom but you'll have to pay for it.

WATER/DRAINAGE

Plumbers: For general advice on plumbing problems, contact the National Federation of Plumbers and Domestic Heating Engineers at Scottish Mutual House, North Street, Hornchurch, Essex.

Floods: Those who live near a river bank may find themselves flooded out of their houses in severe weather conditions. There are several sources of help in such circumstances. The local authority may provide sandbags and help with building barriers, while the fire brigade and police are the people to deal with any rescue which may be required.

Drains: Blocked drains not only cause a nuisance, they could also be a health hazard. First call your local authority. In some areas they may be prepared to clear it for you without charge, but they are entitled to make some charge if they are convinced that the blockage is in some way due to your neglect. You would, of course, only call the local authority in the case of underground, outside drains. If your sink is blocked or the bath water won't drain away then call either a drain clearing firm or your local plumber.

Index

Brass, to clean tarnished 180
Brass curtain tracks, to oil 45
Breadbins:
    to keep clean 88
    to prevent rust in 47
Brocade, care of 124
Broderie anglaise, care of 124
Bronze, removal of green spots on
    180
Bruises, to relieve 250
Bubble bath 74
Building services 268
Bulk buying 64, 65
Bulletin board 49
Bump (fabric), care of 124
Burns, first aid for 247–8
Butter stains, to remove 151
Buttons and buttonholes 19–20

C

Cabbage, to avoid cooking smells
    from 100
Cable grips 230
Calico, care of 124
Cambric, care of 124
Candles:
    to fit into holders 52
    to make last longer 54
    no-smoke wicks 52
    to repair broken 54
Candlewax stains, to remove
    151–2;
    from wallpaper 186
Candlewick, care of 124
Cane seats, to tighten 197
Cane and wicker, to clean 94
Canvas, care of 125
Canvas shoes, care of 200
Car wax or polish stain, to remove
    152
Carbon paper stain, to remove 152
Carpet beetles 107
Carpet off-cuts:
    as cheap or free flooring 202
    uses for 44, 46
Carpet tiles, to clean 90
Carpets:

to clean and shampoo 85–6, 94
    to remove stains from 146
Cast-iron cookware, to clean 180
Cat repellant 59
Ceramic hobs, to clean 95
Ceramic tiles:
    to clean 90
    to remove stains from 181
Chairs:
    care of 197
    to clean 87
    to mend wobbling legs 44, 197–8
Chalk marks to remove 155
Challis, care of 125
Cheesecloth, care of 125
Chemicals, to remove smell oı 103
Chenille, care of 125
Chest, expanding the 252
Chewing gum and stain, to remove
    152–3
Chicken, to buy 66
Chiffon, care of 125
Children, safety with 234–8
Children's clothing, size charts 258
China:
    home-made stain remover for
    177
    to mend 201
Chintz, care of 126
Chocolate stains, to remove 153
Choking, first aid for 250
Chopping board 62; to remove
    smells from 100
Chrome, to clean 95
Chrome cleaner, home-made 178
Cigarette burns on wood furniture,
    to remove 188
Cigarette smoke smell, to remove
    100
Ciré, care of 126
Citizens Advice Bureau 272-3
Clothes:
    care of 40-4
    cleaning labels and codes 118–21
    removing shine from 44
    size charts 258, 259
    washing techniques 210–15
Clutter box 74
Cobwebs, to remove 75
Cockroaches 274
Cocoa stains, to remove 153

279

D

fabric in washing machine 43

E

Earache, relief from 252
Earwigs 108
Egg-boxes as seed boxes 207
Egg cartons, use for 51
Egg stains, to remove 156–7
Elastic, to thread 17
Electric blankets:
    care of 196
    safety precautions with 231–2
Electric cookers, to clean 181
Electrical appliances:
    care of 195–6
    safety with 228–31
Electricity, general information on
    269–70
Electrocution, first aid for 244
Embroidered clothes, to wash 214
Embroidery 20
Embroidery frame, home-made 13
Enamel cookware, to remove
    stains from 182
Eraser, improvised 59
Eucalyptus oil 144
Evening dress, to hang a 40
Extractor fans, to clean 89
Eye, object in the, to remove 250

F

Fahrenheit/Celsius conversions 263
Fainting, first aid for 248–9
Fat, safety with when deep frying
    225
Fat stains, to remove 151
Feather duster 76
Felt, care of 127
Felt-tip pen marks, to remove 157
Fever, first aid for 248
Filter cleaning 193
Finger marks on furniture, to
    remove 189
Fire emergencies, to deal with 270–1

Fire hazards:
    general 227–8
    in the kitchen 225–7
Fireplaces, to cover old 68
Fires:
    to light 57
    paper 'logs' for 70
    to revive 55
First aid 244–53; kit 246
Fish:
    to buy 65
    to remove smell of 101
Fits, first aid for 248
Flannel, care of 128
Flannels:
    to make from bath towels 12
    rinse for 178
Fleas 108, 274
Flexes, maintenance of 192–3
Flies 109–10
Floods 277
Floor mop, rinse for 178
Floorboards:
    to renovate 87
    squeaky 29
Flooring. See also Linoleum etc.
    patterned 202
Flowers:
    care of cut 33–4
    vases for short 59
Fluff remover for clothes 43
Foil, kitchen:
    to re-use 70
    as wrapping paper 57
Food mixers, to clean 75
Food, shopping for economically
    64–5
Freezers:
    care of 194–5
    fillers for 206–7
Frost protectors for plants 58
Fruit:
    to buy 65
    to remove stains caused by
    157–8, 177
Fuel saving 66–7
Fumes, danger from 241
Furnishings, care of 198–9
Furniture. See also Beds etc.
    care of 44–6, 197
    to clean plastic 87
    to clean wood 87, 99

J

Jam stains, to remove 161
Jeans:
  to lengthen 43
  to wash 213
Jersey:
  care of 128
  to sew 14
Jewellery, to clean 42

K

Ketchup stains, to remove 162
Kettles:
  care of 195
  to remove furring 96, 183
Keys, easy to find 57
Kitchen:
  to clean the 88–91
  cutting down chores in
    the 61–3
  fire hazards 225–7
  safety precautions
    in the 224–5
  smells, to remove 100–1
  useful hints 48–52
Knitting hints 8–10
Knitting needles:
  sizes 256
  to straighten 8
Knitting wool:
  to join 9
  to keep tidy 8–9
  to re-use 8
Knives:
  holder for 204
  to sharpen 51
  to store 48

L

Lace care of 128–9
Laminated plastic surfaces, to
  remove stains from 183

Lavatory:
  cistern overflows 28
  to clean the 83
  hygiene in the 243
  to remove stains from the 183
Lawn (fabric), care of 129
Leaks:
  in crockery 201
  in plumbing joints 28
  in vases 201
Leather:
  care of 129–30
  to clean 96
  to remove stains from 184
  upholstery, to clean 87
Leisure wear, to wash 214
Lemon as stain remover 144
Length, to measure 261
Lice 274
Lids, to remove stubborn 50
Linen:
  care of 130
  to prevent yellowing 44
Linings in clothes, to replace 12
Linoleum:
  to clean 96
  tile cleaner 178
Lipstick marks, to remove 162
Liquid cleaners 78
Liquid measures 260
Locks 232–3
  for bathrooms 237
  to free jammed 29
Loft insulation 67
Loose covers, to clean 88

M

Machine sewing tips 13–16
Make-up:
  bags for 200
  to remove stains caused by
    162–3
Marble, to clean 96
Marble tops, polish for 177
Margarine stains, to remove 151
Marmalade stains, to remove 161
Mascara stains, to remove 163

Q

R

S

T

INDEX